HANDWOVEN TAPE

HANDWOVEN TAPE

Understanding and Weaving
Early American and Contemporary Tape

Susan Faulkner Weaver

4880 Lower Valley Road • Atglen, PA 19310

Page 16 image of *Mr. and Mrs. Thomas Mifflin* by John Singleton Copley is used courtesy of the Philadelphia Art Museum. *(125th Anniversary Acquisition. Bequest of Mrs. Esther F. Wistar to The Historical Society of Pennsylvania in 1900, and acquired by the Philadelphia Museum of Art by mutual agreement with the Society through the generosity of Mr. and Mrs. Fitz Eugene Dixon, Jr., and significant contributions from Stephanie S. Eglin, and other donors to the Philadelphia Museum of Art, as well as the George W. Elkins Fund and the W. P. Wilstach Fund, and through the generosity of Maxine and Howard H. Lewis to the Historical Society of Pennsylvania, 1999.)*

Front cover, center photo: These six tapes are shown courtesy of the Collection of Schwenkfelder Library and Heritage Center. From left to right:

Bundle of handwoven indigo blue and bleached white linen tape, ¼" wide, 2-ply, approximately six yards in length. Contains one 20" piece tied around bundle, may have been cut off something and added to bundle. Twelve warp ends, six blue and six white. Blue linen used as weft. Probably from Montgomery or Berks Counties in Pennsylvania.

Bundle of handwoven blue and white tape, ⅝" wide, woven with 2-ply bleached linen and 3-ply indigo cotton. Wrapped in a 5½" long bundle. Inside end was hemmed, the outside end is left raw. Sixteen warp ends, eight each blue and white. White linen used as weft. Bleached linen thread has the look of natural color due to age, but inside it is bright white. Probably from Montgomery or Berks Counties in Pennsylvania.

Bundle of handwoven tape, 5⁄16" wide. Woven of bleached, brown, and natural linen. Bundle is 5" by 1" and about three yards total length. Fifteen warp ends with dark brown used as weft. Probably from southeastern Pennsylvania.

Bundle of handwoven tape, ¼" wide. Blue and red cotton thread and 2-ply bleached linen thread, discolored with age. Tape inside still shows white color. Inside end is hemmed and outer end cut. Wrapped in a 7" by 2½" bundle, approximately eight yards long. Weft is a 2-ply brown linen. Probably from Montgomery or Berks Counties in Pennsylvania.

Small bundle of handwoven blue and white linen tape, ⅛" wide. About four yards total length. Inside end is braided, about four inches. The outside end is cut. Threads are fine 2-ply bleached linen and indigo linen. Twelve warp ends, making a checkerboard pattern. Probably from Montgomery or Berks Counties in Pennsylvania.

Bundle of handwoven indigo blue and bleached linen tape, with red cotton center, ½" wide. Variation of checkerboard pattern. Probably from Montgomery or Berks Counties in Pennsylvania.

Type set in Minion

ISBN: 978-0-7643-5196-9

Printed in China

Published by Schiffer Publishing, Ltd.
4880 Lower Valley Road
Atglen, PA 19310
Phone: (610) 593-1777; Fax: (610) 593-2002
E-mail: Info@schifferbooks.com
Web: www.schifferbooks.com

For our complete selection of fine books on this and related subjects, please visit our website at www.schifferbooks.com. You may also write for a free catalog.

Schiffer Publishing's titles are available at special discounts for bulk purchases for sales promotions or premiums. Special editions, including personalized covers, corporate imprints, and excerpts, can be created in large quantities for special needs. For more information, contact the publisher.

We are always looking for people to write books on new and related subjects. If you have an idea for a book, please contact us at proposals@schifferbooks.com.

Dedication

To my dear son, Stephen Jonathan, who, through his sacrifice,
pointed me into the absorbing world of hand weaving.

To my devoted husband, Jim, with all of his patience
while I was weaving this book together.

To my role model in life, my mother.

And to all the tape weavers, throughout history, who have never been
acknowledged by name, those unknown weavers who wove many, many yards of
handwoven tape for their family needs. I applaud your quiet perseverance.

CONTENTS

Preface

A number of years ago, I worked at a Pennsylvania German living history museum, Landis Valley Village and Farm Museum, formerly Landis Valley Museum, in Lancaster, Pennsylvania. In the textile barn, there was much to learn and explore about the Pennsylvania German culture's textile arts. When I left my position at this museum after seven and a half years, I continued weaving in my studio, Warp Seed Studio. I sold my traditional textiles at museum shops, and wove a variety of other textiles for craft shows and numerous stores.

But the different models of tape looms that I had used at Landis Valley Village and Farm Museum continued to intrigue me. Their function, simplicity of design, and portability created such quiet, peaceful handloom moments. I began doing more research on traditional tape looms and realized, more and more, how extensive the strong, narrow bands were in the family life of many rural settlers of early America. My study of the culture of handwoven tape weaving has developed into this book, to share this fascinating part of craft history with a wider audience.

Acknowledgments

I'm grateful to the many people who helped in making this book a reality:

Jonathan Seidel, whose tape looms helped inspire me to seriously think about the possibilities of writing this book. They are so beautifully crafted that I do not hesitate to suggest them to my tape weaving students, as well as to this book's readers.

Suze Sharpless Messimer, for her expertise and knowledgeable help in the compiling of her handwoven tape collection. I give her a huge and very special thank you. Her contribution to my book is absolutely invaluable, since there is such a limited availability of handwoven tape to study and thoroughly examine. She has had such patience with my numerous visits to her home to complete the study and documentation of her tape collection.

Eleanor Bittle, "The Tape Lady," who kindly consented to be a part of this book. She has so many years of experience with and dedication to handwoven tape of the eighteenth century. I appreciate all of the detailed information that she has shared with me.

Jerry Yancheck, in her steady exploring and collecting of Pennsylvania German textiles and artifacts over the years, has been inspiring. Being a dedicated historical weaver of the eighteenth and nineteenth centuries herself, her Pennsylvania German "drawn work" on "show" towels is absolutely meticulous.

Martha Brunner, my fiber friend for many years, and my model for this book.

Gay McGeary and her in-depth coverlet information.

Chris Yovino from Hagley Museum, Wilmington, Delaware, has been an advocate of box tape looms for a number of years, introducing them to the museum's summer workshops for children.

Candace Perry, curator of collections, Schwenkfelder Library and Heritage Center, Pennsburg, Pennsylvania, for all of her help with special images, including some for the cover of the book.

Jennifer Royer, curator at Landis Valley Village and Farm Museum, Pennsylvania Historical and Museum Commission, Lancaster, Pennsylvania, for her behind-the-scenes tour of their museum's tape loom collection.

Elizabeth Bertheaud, site director of Ephrata Cloister, Ephrata, Pennsylvania, and her devotion to tape weaving.

Becky Gochnauer, director of Hans Herr House and Museum, Willow Street, Pennsylvania, and her assistant, Starla Hess, for their help and assistance.

Linda Eaton, textile curator at Winterthur Museum, Winterthur, Delaware, and her professional staff, Susan F. Newton, and Lea Lane, for all of their patient help.

Zachery Long, tour guide at Daniel Boone Homestead, Birdsboro, Pennsylvania.

Les Stark and all of his important work on the history of hemp in southeastern Pennsylvania.

Mary Jane Myers, quality administrator at Wayne Mills Company, for her in-depth tour of a modern commercial tape mill in Philadelphia, Pennsylvania.

Tom Knisely, former general manager and head instructor of The Mannings Handweaving School and prolific writer of weaving articles and books, who kept chanting, "Get up at five AM and write." He was right! In January 2016, he and his daughter, Sara Bixler, opened Red Stone Glen Fiber Arts Center in York Haven, Pennsylvania.

Lynn Lamont, my cousin from far away, who lent her support in this new writing world.

Sandra Korinchak, my editor in this writing venture. Her calm, straightforward manner has been wonderful guidance and has kept me focused through it all.

And all of the other various museum folks, for whom I had many questions regarding the undocumented history of handwoven tape.

My background is as a craftsperson, a hand weaver. It is my intention to give the reader the texture and color of handwoven tape. Everything written in this book, including any mistakes, are mine and I take full responsibility for them.

Introduction

In our modern world, the little word, "tape," has a multitude of meanings—Scotch tape, duct tape, masking tape, cassette tape, videotape, and the old standard, the tape measure. It is quite an extensive list.

This four-letter word also had different meanings to different groups of people throughout history. Every culture needed long, narrow bands of cloth for their tying and strapping needs. Different cultures have referred to tape in their own manner, and have made it with their own variations in style and appearance. It has been called "tape," "tape ribbon," "band," "inkle," "inkle band," "strap," "belt," "back strap," and "trim."

Handwoven tape forms "the ties that bind," representing the binding together of different cultures and their tape histories. Every tape loom had a story, whether it was in the home of an English, Quaker, Scandinavian, or Pennsylvania German family. Folks in these varied cultures were all weaving tape during the early American period of our history.

Contemporary tape weavers represent the ties that bind the traditional handwoven tape from early America to today, through their work of replicating, embellishing, and evolving the original tape patterns to be part of our modern age.

Oral traditions were important for passing down the early Americans' common tape patterns. The looms were handmade, and the many weavers of tape provided the handwoven tape needed by the family households. This is the account of the utilitarian hand-loomed tape used for so many ties, in so many lives.

The Pennsylvania German culture in the new colonies played an important craft role in the making of their decorative arts, which included their handwoven tape. By discovering and researching their most interesting tape history, I realized the Pennsylvania Germans were the source of much of the American hand-loomed tape weaving that we know about today.

Living for many years in southeastern Pennsylvania, I have been fortunate to have learned about the local Pennsylvania German history and traditions. Marrying a man from Pennsylvania German heritage has also given me insight into their culture, as well as their current day-to-day living. My husband's family, from Lebanon County, Pennsylvania, migrated to America as Reformed Lutherans, sometimes referred to as the "Gay Dutch." They were the Pennsylvania Germans that were the non-Amish, Mennonite, and Brethren Plain groups. They lived rurally in farming communities. My mother-in-law grew up on a farm in Fredericksburg, Pennsylvania, growing tomatoes for the Campbell Soup Company.

As a hand weaver, I have been drawn to historical handwoven textiles for many years. It wasn't until I began working as a fiber educator in the textile barn of Landis Valley Village and Farm Museum that I developed a deep curiosity and interest in handwoven tape. This Pennsylvania German museum introduced me to tape, tape looms, and the history of these strong narrow bands. I discovered the important role that tape played in everyday lives, throughout many generations, first in Europe, and then in America. It was my responsibility to educate the visitors to the fiber world of the mid eighteenth and early nineteenth centuries in America. I would also demonstrate the spinning of flax on the flax wheel, weave cloth on the barn loom, and weave tape, which included weaving tape for the costumes of the interpreters. I was fortunate to be able to explore the history and making of tape and the more I learned about it, the more fascinated I became with the variety of its uses and the family tape culture in the rural households.

There was something about these simple tape looms that attracted me to them. I may have gotten a little carried away with creating tape projects for myself while working at the museum. I wove tape for the entire separation "rope" that separated the staff and visitors in the very large room of the textile barn. This way the visitors would be able to see and feel the tape, as I described and demonstrated the weaving of these narrow bands. Another project I gave myself was in the textile dye gardens, just outside the barn doors. Colorful tape worked wonderfully to stake up the different plants as they grew. Over the summer the tape might get a little faded from the sun, but it still kept its pattern and function.

Hand-loomed tapes were necessary for many families during the colonial time in America, from New England down to the southern colonies. Part One of this book is focused on traditional handwoven tapes of the past—that is, functional, utilitarian tying and strapping tape, used for such things as clothes ties and satchel straps.

Throughout this book, I use the terms "colonial" and "early American" interchangeably. These terms are used here in a general interpretative way; I am not distinguishing the specific time periods, but am focusing instead on a time I am calling the "American colonial era" that runs approximately from the early 1700s to the early 1800s.

Handwoven tape was very important throughout Europe from the sixteenth century on and continuing into the early American colonies, to the mid-nineteenth century. A part of everyday life, most family members needed tape for their personal use, for tying their clothing, such as drawstrings to hold up women's petticoats, pocket ties, and garters for holding up men and women's stockings. There was no elastic or zippers in the colonial period of America! Utilitarian tape was also a necessity for such items as candle wicks, wagon cover ties, grain and feed bag ties, and all kinds of satchel strapping.

Most farm households had their own tape loom, with the tape hand woven by the family members. It was woven in this way and sometimes sold commercially up to the 1850s, when textile mills took over the tape weaving process. There were three different models of tape looms: the paddle, lap, or knee tape loom; the box tape loom; and the standing or floor tape loom. Each of these looms made it possible for the weaver to weave off many yards of tape for the family needs.

When many historians think of "tape," they may be focusing on the "fancy tape" or "trim," which was commercially milled and available for those who could afford to buy it. Much of it was shipped into the colonies from England and was used as decorative accents or to trim furniture upholstery, pillows, and curtains, or used as seam binding. There certainly was a vast array of "trim" tape in early America, and it was quite impressive in its elaborateness. It is mentioned in this book, but only briefly. That research is for someone else. If you're seeking an in-depth account of "trim tape," this isn't the book you're looking for.

My exploration of early American handwoven tape considers the tape history of several European cultures, as well as southeastern Pennsylvania and the tape weaving culture of the Pennsylvania Germans. I have identified the Pennsylvania German tape culture specifically whenever possible, since this is where I have based my study.

There are very few books written that give an in-depth account of hand-loomed tape traditions from the eighteenth and nineteenth centuries in early America. Even Ellen J. Gehret comments several times in her book, *Rural Pennsylvania Clothing,* that tapes were so seldom mentioned in the early records of the Pennsylvania Germans and that early references seldom elaborate beyond the word "tape," without a breakdown of usage. In her discussion on tape garters, hand-loomed tape used to "keep the stocking in place, was evidently such a common and minute part of the Pennsylvania men's and women's wardrobe that it was not given importance or value in wills and inventories—it is seldom listed."[1]

Without solid documentation, it is impossible to actually identify tape woven by a certain weaver. Tape weavers, for the most part, were unknown weavers. Therefore, in many cases, the exact history of a particular bundle of tape cannot be tracked, tape being such a common textile item used in a wide region. Clarke Hess, in his book *Mennonite Arts,* does have a little documentation on tape and tape looms, stemming from the Mennonite culture of the local southeastern Pennsylvania region, with the written history passed down through the generations. Historical museums may have their tape collections documented, to a degree. But, if tape is found at a flea market or at an auction, more than likely there would be no documentation of that tape. So the mystery continues.

Having said all of that, I am very proud of the extensive collection of hand-loomed tape that I am presenting in this book, the Historical Tape Pattern Directory, in Chapter 4. Even though

Tape Tales

In the beginning of each chapter, I've written a little tale or glimpse into the colonial past, as well as a couple of "Tape Tales" in today's times. Each tale is a fictional story revolving around family tape weaving activities. These are imaginary flashbacks, based on historical records of day-to-day household weaving. I created these Tape Tales to serve as a thread tying together families and the different chapter topics.

there is no documentation regarding the exact location where the tape was woven, nor the name of the weaver, the owner of this tape collection does name the circumstances whereby she obtained the individual pieces of tape. I was very fortunate to be given the opportunity to examine these tapes in detail. The tape in this valuable collection has information that can be used for replication, as well as simply allowing us a better understanding of the characteristics of the individual tapes. The photographs of this entire collection were taken by Morgan Beye, former photo editor at Schiffer Publishing, and they are outstanding. The sharp clarity really enables the reader to view the detail of these narrow bands.

The assortment of other photos of tape and the historical tape looms in this book were, for the most part, taken in the southeastern Pennsylvania region, consisting of Berks, Bucks, Chester, Lancaster, Lebanon, Montgomery, and York Counties.

Part Two contains how-to instructions, and projects for today's weavers to try. When I first began thinking about writing this book, I was only considering the historical aspects of hand-woven tape of early America. Being a hand weaver and a weaving instructor, though, I realized that there would be people who might actually enjoy the "how to" of tape weaving and of actually replicating the old patterns or creating their own new ones. Weaving on a historical tape loom can be a humbling feeling, as you become a part of the loom's past, knowing that there were probably others that used the same loom to weave yards of tape, probably for their families.

As I was writing this book, I watched it slowly grow and take shape, as a weaving develops on the loom, gathering in body, color, texture, and length. Throughout the process, my goal has been to inspire people to explore handwoven tape and the traditional tape looms. The history is quite engaging, with the family being the thread that kept the tape on the loom.

For reenactors and docents, there is a lot of interesting information here that can be shared with museum visitors. And for hand weavers, I hope my book leads to exploring some of the traditional, as well as contemporary, tape patterns, and the enjoyment of weaving many narrow bands of tape for functional and decorative projects.

PART ONE

Eighteenth- & Early Nineteenth-Century American Handwoven Tape, with a Focus *on the* Pennsylvania German Culture

1. Historical Overview of Handwoven Tape in Early America

The Move to America

During the eighteenth and early nineteenth centuries, many European cultural groups were making long and arduous migrations from the Old World of Europe to the new settlements in America. As a part of these migrations, people from a variety of different cultures began settling into the southeastern region of Pennsylvania. In 1681, William Penn was granted, from King James II, an immense tract of land west of the Delaware River. A variety of European cultures, the English, Scotch-Irish, Swiss, and Germans, moved into this region, as well as into other areas of Pennsylvania and surrounding states, bringing their different religions with them. There were Lutherans, Quakers, Moravians, Jews, Mennonites, and Amish.

A traditional tape loom and tape. In background, Lancaster County, Pennsylvania, box tape loom from 1790–1850, which I purchased from Eleanor Bittle, "The Tape Lady." On right, checked linen apron with linen tape ties. Handmade rye straw basket filled with wooden tape holders and variety of traditional handwoven tape. Several bundles of tape, to the left. *Loom belongs to author. Tape, basket and apron appear in Historical Tape Pattern Directory, tape collection belonging to Susan Sharpless Messimer.*

Whether escaping from religious persecution, leaving behind personal turmoil, or looking for economic gain, waves of immigrants came into this southeastern Pennsylvania region. The Pennsylvania Germans, included in these migrations, immigrated from the Palatinate, Rhineland in modern Germany, Switzerland, Austria, Czechoslovakia, and France. The majority of German immigrants were farmers and lived off the land, in their rural homesteads. By the time of the American Revolution, about 90% of American people lived on farms.[1] The combination of self-sufficiency and having a variety of professional craftspeople was crucial to their daily lives.

Along the middle Atlantic coast, Philadelphia, Pennsylvania, and Baltimore, Maryland, became the two hubs for commercial trade. Outlying urban centers were still in their infancy.

My Tape Ties
Tape Tale #1

Waking up on a cold, gray morning, I realize I am going to be late for work. "It takes so long to get dressed," I grumble to myself. Layer upon layer of clothing to put on gets very tedious. Because of the cold, I'll have to put on a few more petticoats for warmth. Tying, tying, tying all this tape to make them fit around my waist. The straight pins are so slow to fasten my short gown, and usually prick my finger in the process. My woolen scarf requires an even larger straight pin. Where did I put it? Then, my long stockings, coming up above my knees, are quite woolly warm, but mean more tape ties for my garters, to keep them up. If I can find my buckled shoes, I'll be ready to wrap up in my blanket cape and dash off to my job. Every work day, so many tape ties that bind me to my clothes. One of the most time-consuming features of working in a living history Pennsylvania German museum is getting tied into my 1790 costume and then climbing out of it at the end of the day, *un*tying all of those tape ties. Makes me really appreciate zippers, buttons, and Velcro!

Weaving Differences between the English and Pennsylvania German Communities

In the English culture, houses were generally larger than the smaller log houses of the German immigrants. Having more space accommodated the family barn loom, either a two- or four-harness barn loom. These looms were quite large, usually more than 40 inches in width alone. Sometimes the barn loom would have been kept in the attic or a shed-loft. The household linens and woolens were spun and woven by the women settlers in the English tradition, hence the term "homespun industries."[2]

General stores were another source for the family cloth. After 1750, imported foreign fabric could be purchased there or from the peddlers passing by, to help supplement what the English women were producing themselves in their homes.

By the late 1700s, stores were purchasing "trimmings" that were commercially made in England and brought to the colonies for sale. Store owners would buy these textiles in Baltimore and Philadelphia for their shops farther in from the coast. "Trimmings" included ribbons and tapes for embellishing clothing. Decorative and ornamental, the commercial "trim" could be used as upholstery tape for furniture, seam binding, and curtain and carpet binding, as well.

As opposed to the rural farm women working their new land with their families, the fashionable English housewife in America might have had her own little box tape loom, and it may have been quite fancy in decoration. It would have been called a "trim," "parlor," or "fringe" loom and would have been used for fine and fancy trim, possibly for a small project, such as trim around a pocketbook or a pillow. More so than for functional ties, like those that the farming settlers were producing, the English housewife could have woven on her loom as a fashion statement of the day, or as a "hobbyist." Weaving on her tape loom could have been a political statement, displaying her frugality during the big push for domestically produced goods in the Revolutionary War period.[3]

When tapes and ribbons were much more scarce than in today's world, these small portable looms were quite popular. Whether used by a wealthy English housewife or a rural farm wife, from sleek and fancy looms to the more primitive, the looms all made tape. There was an interesting variety of names for these little looms—tape looms, braid looms, belt looms, garter looms or "gallus-frames."[4]

The German, Swiss, English, and other cultures all contributed to a variety of choices in textiles. It really depended on one's station in life, whether tape was made at home, for fancy finery or function, or commercially woven, bought by those who could afford it in the store. There was the blending between homespun and store bought fabrics, between the simple to the bright and shiny, and that included tape. Very narrow tapes were woven for tying. The wider tapes were used for straps and binding, and there were fancier edgings, such as fringe. For pictures of handwo-

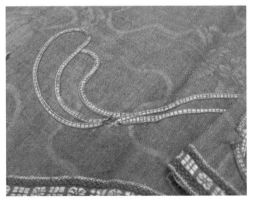

Tan tape on a valance. 1775–1800, New England. Colonial English "trim" tape applied to linen fabric. *Collection of Winterthur Museum.*

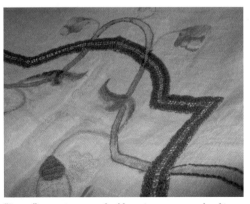

"Fancy" green tape on a bed hanging, an example of Colonial English "trim" applied to fabric. 1750–1800, Boston. *Collection of Winterthur Museum. Museum purchase with funds provided by special fund for Collection Objects.*

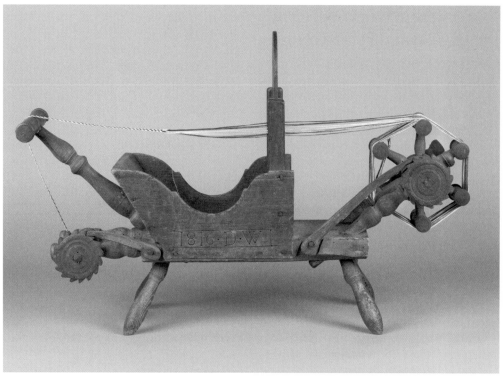

Tape loom, 1816, Pennsylvania. Maple, white pine, tulip poplar, ash. *Courtesy of Winterthur Museum. Museum purchase with funds drawn from the Centenary Fund.*

Eleanor Bittle, "The Tape Lady"

Ever since I had become interested in handwoven tape, I had heard of Eleanor Bittle, "The Tape Lady." Her reputation preceded our actually meeting. Once I met her, I realized what a delightful lady she is, very passionate about eightenth-century American history, specifically early linen tape weaving. Since 1976, she has been active in numerous roles at the Peter Wentz Farmstead in Worcester, Pennsylvania. As one of the first history interpreters there, she has remained diligent in her ongoing study and research into the history of tape loom weaving. Eleanor has amassed a large collection of the various models of tape looms, and she has donated many of her looms to museums, including Mercer Museum in Doylestown, Pennsylvania, and Winterthur in Winterthur, Delaware. She enjoys educating others and sharing information about the historical tape traditions, and she conducts colonial period demonstrations on tape weaving to a variety of children's and adult groups in the area. She can be found every year at the Goschenhoppen Folk Festival in Green Lane, Pennsylvania. I feel very honored to have spent time with this special lady, exploring historical tape with her.

"The Tape Lady" plaque, made by Eleanor Bittle; she took it along with her for many years, when demonstrating her tape weaving skills. *Collection of Eleanor Bittle, The Tape Lady ©.*

ven and commercially woven balanced plain weave tapes from this era, see pages 91 and 108.

Pennsylvania German Family Tape Weaving Culture

Compared to the English way, the Pennsylvania Germans' cloth was woven from a different tradition. Their log homes were small and filled with many family members. There was no extra room for a large barn loom. Being quite self-sufficient, nearly every Pennsylvania German family had its own flax and hemp patch to supply their raw materials for hand spinning of linen and hemp thread. Wool from the family's herd of sheep was also needed for spinning and weaving their family textiles. The women and girls spent a great deal of time spinning their thread, but the yard goods needed for their clothing, household linens, and agricultural cloth (such as feed bags) were handwoven by the professional weavers. The family would give the weaver many skeins of their handspun yarn, arranging for certain amounts

Typical eighteenth-century barn loom, traditionally used by professional village weavers in southeastern Pennsylvania. This working artifact is on display at Landis Valley Village and Farm Museum, Lancaster. I'm shown here in period clothing, weaving hand-loomed cloth. Oops—where's my linen cap?

and patterns of fabric to be woven. Bartering was used during this period, so the family's handwo-

---

Sarah Mifflin Weaving Fringe on a Tape "Fringe" Loom

The portrait Mr. and Mrs. Thomas Mifflin was painted by the successful American portrait painter John Singleton Copley, who lived from 1738 to 1815. When the portrait was painted, in 1773, Thomas Mifflin was a wealthy Philadelphia merchant. His Quaker wife, Sarah, was twenty-six years old.

In an article for McCalls Aline Saarinen writes, "Unquestionably, the Mifflin portrait is one of Copley's triumphs. He ingeniously held the composition together by using the hands as a hub. He gave the faces equal importance." She goes on, "The characterizations are convincing: Sarah Mifflin, at her fringe loom, seems alert, firm, upstanding; her husband, attractive, warm, extroverted; their prosperous station underscored by the handsome clothes, the finely turned spider-leg table. The picture has, simultaneously, immediacy and timelessness."[5]

Governor of Pennsylvania from 1790 to 1799, Thomas Mifflin lived a lavish lifestyle, costing him the governorship, and he died a pauper.

Today the portrait is housed at the Philadelphia Art Museum.

Mr. and Mrs. Thomas Mifflin, painted by John Singleton Copley in 1773. This famous portrait of Pennsylvania Governor Mifflin and his wife, Sarah, seen weaving tape fringe, has perked the attention of many hand weavers. She most likely was not actually weaving tape fringe, but simply holding it for the portrait. Courtesy of the Philadelphia Art Museum. See copyright page for further credit information.

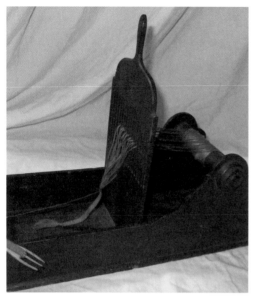

Small box tape loom, bought by Eleanor Bittle from dealer in Lancaster County, Pennsylvania. Handwoven silk tape on loom woven by Eleanor Bittle, with fish netter as her shuttle. *Collection of Eleanor Bittle, The Tape Lady ©.*

Weaving tape on simple box tape loom from Lancaster County, Pennsylvania. *Martha Brunner, weaver and model. Collection of author.*

ven cloth could have been bartered for the weaver's firewood, for example.

The professional weavers, who were usually men, were part of the area's Pennsylvania German agricultural-craft economy.[6] The craft guilds were carried over from the Old World, with young people apprenticing in different crafts. These weavers would also have their own farms to tend to, so most often they would do their weaving during the winter months, taking orders for cloth from the farm families in their area.

Children Weaving Tape in the Field

"When it was necessary to tend the sheep in the fields, the children and others had a lot of leisure time. So, they could 'be set to some other employment whithal, such as spinning upon the rock, knitting, weaving tape, etc.'"

—Alice Morse Earle,
Home Life in Colonial Days, 1898

In *Rural Pennsylvania Clothing*, Ellen Gehret describes the functional tapes for everyday use. "Many narrow tapes, including men's and women's garters, were produced in the home in varying widths utilized in wearing apparel, for household and bed linens, and in agriculture and the trades."[7]

Historically, handwoven tape was not generally documented, either individually or in the family. Tape was seldom listed in wills and inventories. It was "such a common and minute part of Pennsylvania men's and women's wardrobe that it was not given importance or value in wills and inventories. It is seldom listed." Gehret goes on to state, "These products of the small tape loom are seldom mentioned in account books or similar records."[8]

Large amounts of tape would most likely have been needed on the farm, especially as the families grew in number. Many family members could have been involved in the family tape weaving. The husband or father could have made the family loom, or it could have been bought in the village store. The women and older children would have been responsible for setting up the tape loom and they, along with the elders, would have woven a great deal of the family tape. Children possibly as young as six years old could also have helped weave the tape, giving them an easy job and keeping them away from their mother's busy household chores.

Eleanor Bittle agrees that it was probably the young children and the older family members, the grandparents, who were the primary tape weavers of the family. (See Chapter 4 for more information regarding Eleanor Bittle and her tape weaving.) In a typical household, farm life was difficult and demanding and everyone had chores, no matter their age. Older people could have helped weave the homespun tape as one way of remaining productive in the family.

The family members, taking turns, may have woven one long tape on their loom, or they could have periodically cut off a section, possibly for a certain project. In most cases, they wove yardage and then determined the uses, as needed. As can be seen in Chapter 4, tape bundles were wrapped after weaving many yards.

It's possible that tape could have been woven in moments of relaxing from some of the other, more strenuous chores. There was probably more tape woven in the winter months, when the weather made it harder to work outside.

Girls Carried Their Tape Looms for a Visit

"Girls carried their tape looms to a neighbor's house for an afternoon's work, just as they did their knitting needles and ball of yarn. A fringe loom might also be occasionally found, for weaving decorative fringes; these were more common in the Hudson River valley than elsewhere."

—Alice Morse Earle,
Home Life in Colonial Days, 1898

Three bundles of tape from the Historical Tape Pattern Collection. *Collection of Susan Sharpless Messimer.*

Traditional Uses of Hand-Loomed Tape

Narrow tape was a very important part of the fastening process for clothing in early American days, since there were no zippers, no safety pins, no elastic, and no Velcro. And buttons were expensive for farm families. Ellen Gehret has written extensively about the typical rural garments worn in southeastern Pennsylvania. She also covers the larger area of Pennsylvania and other surrounding states from 1750 to 1820, with the advent of the Industrial Revolution in America. Her technical editor, Janet Gray Crosson, describes in the foreword of *Rural Pennsylvania Clothing*:

> *The cultural patterns of the German-speaking immigrants to Pennsylvania were not soon abandoned in the New World. The Pennsylvanian scene differed from much of New England, tidewater Maryland and other coastal areas to the south, which were settled by an influx of immigrants from the British Isles. Among clothing, it is known some garments were more or less universal cut, with little ethnic distinctions, but other items of apparel surely possessed characteristics contributed by middle-class Swiss and Palatinates. The clothing of rural Pennsylvania possessed some unique qualities; a distinction should be made between this region and the other colonies when apparel is being considered.[9]*

———

A Great Variety of Tapes

"A study of tapes on garments from [this] period indicates a great variety of widths, weight, colors and designs. But because early references seldom elaborate beyond 'tape,' it has not yet been determined if there was a distinction made between tapes for apparel and tapes used on household linens, bedding and for agricultural purposes, such as ties for seed and grain bags."

—Ellen J. Gehret, *Rural Pennsylvania Clothing*, 1976

———

Period clothing worn during the eighteenth and early nineteenth centuries, by rural women in the southeastern Pennsylvania region. Linsey-woolsey petticoat is hand woven. Apron and bleached linen tape ties attached to woman's cap hand woven by author. *Martha Brunner, model.*

Women's Clothing

Clothing worn by women during these colonial times was generally held together by tying, usually with tape. Or, as in the front of some shortgowns, clothing could be pinned with straight pins.[10] Eleanor Bittle has commented, "Rural southeastern Pennsylvanians were not interested in tape colors matching their clothes. Whatever they had, they'd use. 'This will do. It has to function as I need it.'"[11] As with other needs in their culture, function came first.

Tape Ties for Women's Linen Caps

Women always wore caps during the eighteenth century. One would never see a bare head! The caps worn were usually made of handwoven bleached linen. There were several ways to fasten the cap under the chin, such as buttons, ribbons, or tape ties.[12]

While I was working at Landis Valley Village and Farm Museum, the linen caps worn by some of the women interpreters had a one-eighth-inch, bleached linen tape for tying. As one of the weavers

Close-up of bleached linen tape ties attached to woman's cap. Tape ties hand woven by author. *Martha Brunner, model.*

Standing floor tape loom had been used as working artifact for number of years in textile barn at Landis Valley Village and Farm Museum. When I worked there, it was used solely for weaving of bleached linen tape on women's linen caps. Loom now housed in Collection Building on site, with bleached linen thread still on it, waiting to be woven. *Collection of Landis Valley Village and Farm Museum, Pennsylvania Historical and Museum Commission.*

in the textile barn, I would weave these tapes on the standing, or floor, tape loom pictured here, which at the time was a working artifact. It is presently in the Collection Building at Landis Valley Village and Farm Museum.

Tape Ties for Women's Petticoats

The petticoat of the eighteenth century is the skirt of today. Women wore many petticoats, especially during the winter months, for added warmth. Tape ties could be hand sewn to the top band of the petticoat, to tie around the waist. Many times there would be a hand-sewn waistband and button. At Landis Valley Village and Farm Museum, in many instances, the interpreter's petticoat tape

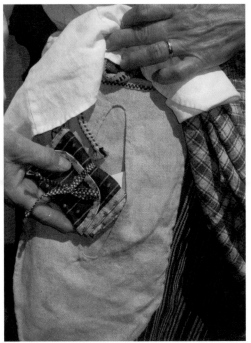

Reproduced tape used for several applications. At top, directly above linen pocket is a bit of tape holding up a woman's linsey-woolsey petticoat. Underneath, piece of pocket tape, wrapped around the waist to hold it on. Being put into pocket is cocalico cotton "housewife" with linen tape tying it together. Three tape pieces hand woven by author and friend.

was a simple drawstring pulled through a petticoat's waistband and around the woman's waist.

Tape Ties for Women's Pockets

The pocket was an accessory to carry personal items, such as hankies, scissors, and the woman's "housewife." There were no pockets sewn into the petticoat, so tape ties were needed to tie the pocket around the woman's waist. It was rarely shown, and was tied underneath the apron or petticoat. As with handwoven tape itself, the pocket was not often mentioned in women's estates or wills.[13]

According to Ellen Gehret, there were three ways that tape was attached to the pocket:
- Tape was whip-stitched on the back of pocket, at edges.
- Tape was folded over top of waistband—wider tape.
- Tape was inserted between the two layers, when finishing the pocket.[14]

Reproduced woman's pocket, hand embroidered, Lancaster County, Pennsylvania, motif, by author. (Sadly, this linen pocket wore out with use, while working at Landis Valley Village and Farm Museum, so its tape ties were cut off and used for other tape tie needs.)

Lady's pocket, front, linen, wool, cotton. 1740–1775, United States. Tape tie woven of natural and indigo blue dyed linen. Tape tie is only on one side. *Courtesy of Winterthur Museum. Bequest of Henry Francis du Pont.*

Lady's pocket, back. Showing tape hand sewn across top. *Courtesy of Winterthur Museum.*

Lady's pocket, back. *Courtesy of Winterthur Museum.*

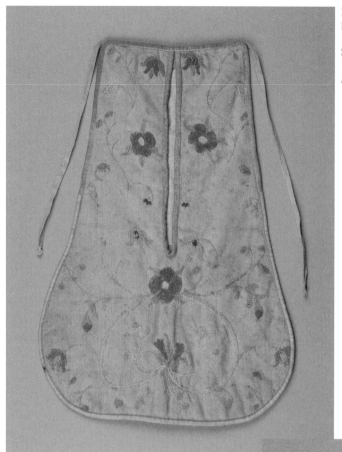

Lady's pocket, front. Wool, linen. 1750–1760, United States. *Courtesy of Winterthur Museum.*

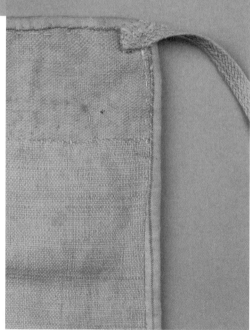

Lady's pocket, back. Notice natural linen tape turned under and hand sewn to back corner of linen pocket. *Courtesy of Winterthur Museum. Bequest of Henry Francis du Pont.*

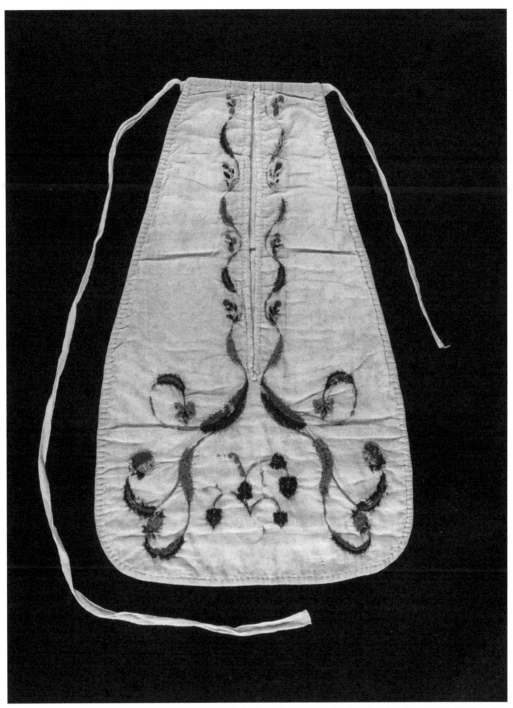

Linen pocket with wool crewel embroidery and initials "SY" on the reverse side. Attributed to Susanna Yeakle (possibly 1782–1861), Chestnut Hill, Montgomery County, Pennsylvana. Notice the two lengths of ties. *Collection of Schwenkfelder Library and Heritage Center.*

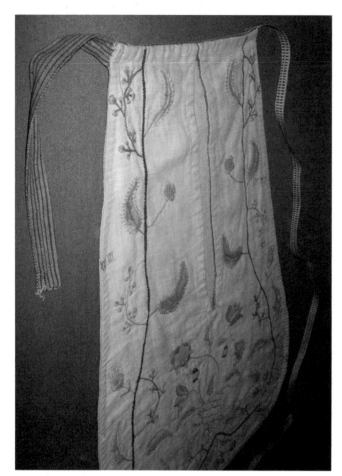

Woman's pocket, embroidered. Wool and silk on linen. Notice tape ties of two different patterns and lengths. Tape tie on left appears much wider than one on right. *Collection of Winterthur Museum. Artifact of the recent acquisitions from estate of legendary collector and scholar Frederick S. Weiser to Winterthur Museum. Bequest of Henry Francis du Pont.*

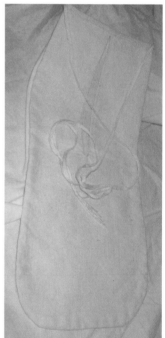

Woman's linen pocket, with handwoven linen tape ties. *Collection of Eleanor Bittle, The Tape Lady ©.*

Reproduced cocalico cotton "housewife" as it appears opened, showing different compartments for housing sewing needs. Attached natural linen and indigo blue dyed tape is checkerboard pattern.

Reproduced linen and wool "housewife," handmade and-handwoven tape by Tom Martin. *Collection of Susan Sharpless Messimer.*

Three reproduced colonial "housewives" with their tape ties. Top and right: depicting eighteenth century plaid and wood block printed cloth. Left: early nineteenth century cocalico cotton, handmade and -woven tape, by Susan Kelleher.

A number of pockets consisted of two tapes of different lengths, at each side of the pocket. This was a practical way of tying on the pocket: the longer tape tie went around the waist and met the shorter tie at the woman's hip.

Many pocket tapes were hand woven and hand sewn. If one could afford it, a fancy pocket could be bought at the general store or in a larger city.

Tape Ties for the Women's "Housewife"

Inside the pocket, the woman's "housewife" or "thread case" could be kept. The "housewife" was tied with tape, and when unrolled, there would be several small sections for storing sewing and embroidery threads and needles. (See the photo on page 21, which shows a "housewife" going into a woman's pocket.)

Tape for Pin Holders

In the colonies, there were a variety of pin cushions, including handwoven, handsewn, and commercial tape that would surround the cushion.

Handcrafted pincushions of cotton fabric, stuffed with wool. Cotton and linen tape hand sewn around pincushion, for hanging. Fabric and tape both hand woven by author.

Handcrafted pin ball by Susan Kelleher. Handwoven linen pin ball in the style of eighteenth and early nineteenth centuries. This design is found on early samples and show towels from the Lancaster County, Pennsylvania, area. *Collection of Susan Sharpless Messimer.*

Handcrafted pin ball made of wrapped silk tape. Could have been used for a lady's favorite hatpins. *Collection of Eleanor Bittle, The Tape Lady ©.*

Tape Ties for Women's Aprons

The apron was a very important part of the clothing worn by rural farmwives in the eighteenth century. Women would typically have several aprons and they were used for numerous purposes. An apron protected the petticoat, but could also carry items, or be used for fanning oneself from the heat. As Ellen Gehret states, "Hand-loomed tape was generally used for the waistband or ties or both. The tape was inserted into a casing, or folded in half and stitched on both sides over the raw gathered top edge of the apron or stitched on top of tiny stroke gathers."[15] Store bought tapes were commercially woven and shipped from England to Philadelphia; and from there, to back country merchants. (See the photo on page 31, which shows an apron with ties attached to the waistband.)

In 1797, when purchasing goods in Philadelphia, a merchant from Lewistown, Pennsylvania, noted that apron tapes would be bought by the dozen.[16]

On the Pennsylvania German farms, folk beliefs and superstitions were a constant. When working at LVV, I took one superstition to heart when putting on my 1790s period outfit. "Accidentally putting on one's apron wrong side out is lucky, but turning it will bring accident or misfortune."[17]

Reproduced apron tape ties of cotton, with pocket tape tie of cotton peeking out on the side. Hand woven by author. *Martha Brunner, model.*

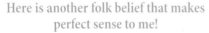

Here is another folk belief that makes perfect sense to me!

"If you lose your garter, it shows your lover is thinking of you."

—Edwin Miller Fogel, *Beliefs and Superstitions of the Pennsylvania Germans*, 1915, as cited by Ellen Gehret, *Rural Pennsylvania Clothing*, 1976.

Tape Garters for All

Tape garters were interesting pieces of apparel. Used as a pair, they would hold up the long stockings, worn by men, women, boys and girls. Since there was no elastic to hold up one's stockings during this time, garter tapes were tied, either above or below the knees. "A fancy and elaborate garter was known to be worn by the affluent during the eighteenth century, but this type of

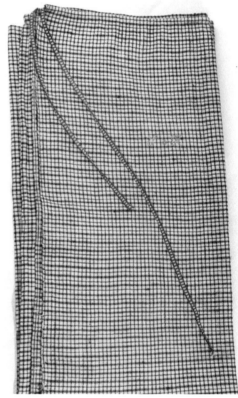

Lady's handstitched apron comprised of handspun blue and bleached white woven checked linen. Near waistline are cross-stitched initials "S.K." in pink (faded red) silk script lettering. Apron has a drawstring waist with ties made of red cotton and blue and bleached white linen handwoven tape. Year range is from 1820–1826. Towamencin Township, Montgomery County, Pennsylvania. *Collection of Schwenkfelder Library and Heritage Center.*

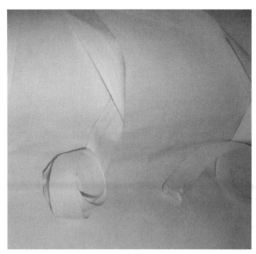

Woman's linen bib apron with commercially woven twill tape ties, hemmed at the bottoms. *Collection of Landis Valley Village and Farm Museum, Pennsylvania Historical and Museum Commission.*

Woman's linen apron with commercially woven cotton waistband. Handwoven linen tape ties sewn to waistband. *Collection of Landis Valley Village and Farm Museum, Pennsylvania Historical and Museum Commission.*

garter was not commonly worn by a Pennsylvanian yeoman as he went about his daily chores. Garters were mentioned in store inventories and ledgers in Pennsylvania. (According to a store record of 1773, at a Lititz store, in southeastern Pennsylvania,) "there were fourteen pairs of garters in stock in the store."[18] The usual garter in the rural areas was of homespun hand-loomed linen tape, probably woven on a tape loom by either the children or the grandparents of the family.

A Little Tape for Men
Men's Suspenders

The manner that suspenders were worn by men in early America, as well as today in the Amish communities, tells much about the group that each man was/is affiliated with. There have been many choices made, such as color, whether the suspenders go straight down or cross in the back, and where they cross. Suspenders, too, could have been handwoven by the rural farmer families or bought in the local store.

Reproduced tape garter used for holding up women's stockings. *Martha Brunner, model.*

Tape Ties for Men's Breeches

On the back of a pair of men's breeches, the gusset would be tied with a thin band of tape. By gathering the fabric with the tape, the waistband could be adjusted.[19]

Tape Holder for Eye Spectacles

According to Ellen Gehret, young men never wore spectacles in public.[20]

Tape Ties for Men's Wallets

Any money would have been carried in needleworked and tooled leather wallets, by both men and women. Men would usually have their wallet in their coat pockets.

Women could hide their wallet in their pocket, hidden under their petticoats. The needleworked wallet would be tied shut with commercially woven tape.[21]

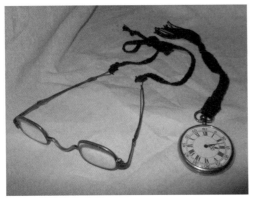

Reproduced linen tape straps for man's pocketwatch and eyeglasses, hand woven by Eleanor Bittle. *Collection of Eleanor Bittle, The Tape Lady* ©.

Reproduction, man's wallet, created in wool, with silk lining. Made in 1981 by Mark Bucco, volunteer at Peter Wentz Farmstead, Worcester, Pennsylvania. Wool tape trim woven by Eleanor Bittle. *Collection of Eleanor Bittle, The Tape Lady* ©.

Pocketbook, wool, silk, linen, cotton, cardboard, felt. 1750–1775, England. *Courtesy of Winterthur Museum. Bequest of Henry Francis du Pont.*

Pocketbook, back. *Courtesy of Winterthur Museum.*

Pocketbook, back corner. *Courtesy of Winterthur Museum.*

Pocketbook, front, with the flap opened. Notice the tape fringe, consisting of tape header with wool fringe, on both sides. See page 114 for more information about this type of tape fringe making. *Courtesy of Winterthur Museum.*

Tape for Household Uses

These samples show some of the common, everyday uses for early American household tape.

Tool Hangers (Tape Loops Tied to End of a Handle)
(See page 160 for examples.)

Candle and Lantern Wicks

Modern candle and lantern wicks of cotton tape. Very similar in appearance to traditional linen and cotton wicks used during eighteenth and early nineteenth centuries.

Seed Bag Ties

Reproduced check and plaid cotton seed bags with linen tape ties, hand woven by Eleanor Bittle. *Courtesy of Eleanor Bittle, The Tape Lady ©.*

Bag and Satchel Straps

On left, reproduced tow bag with linen tape tie, hand woven by friend of author. On right, reproduced plaid cotton satchel with linen tape straps, hand woven by author.

Cradle Lacing Tape

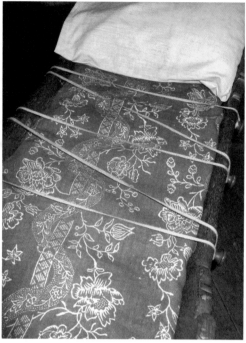

Antique baby cradle with linen lacing tape, hand woven by author, wrapped around the top to keep the baby in place. *Collection of Hans Herr House and Museum.*

Handwoven cradle lacing tape wrapped around historic wooden cradle. The cradle is dated 1789 and probably from Lancaster County, Pennsylvania. *Collection of Winterthur Museum. On loan from David A. Schorsch and Eileen M. Smiles.*

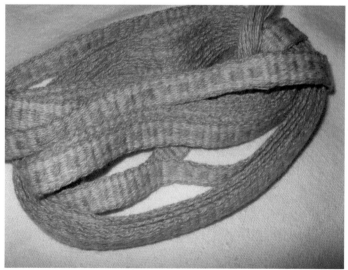

Close-up of tape shown above left. *Collection of Hans Herr House and Museum.*

Bed Linen Ties
(See more in Chapter 4, Historical Tape Pattern Directory.)

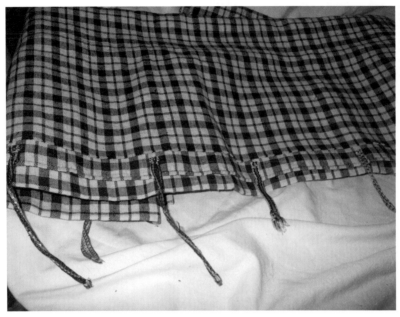

Handwoven plaid linen bed case of bleached linen and indigo blue, with five handwoven linen tape ties. Notice that each tape tie has a different pattern. *Collection of Eleanor Bittle, The Tape Lady ©.*

Pillow Bolster Ties
(See examples in Chapter 4, Historical Tape Pattern Directory.)

Coverlet Tape Fringe
(See more in Chapter 4, Historical Tape Pattern Directory.)

Coverlet of wool and cotton, from 1838, with attached, handwoven tape fringe hand sewn around three sides. (See page 110 for more examples of coverlet tape fringe.) *Collection of the Schwenkfelder Library and Heritage Center.*

Towel Tape Tabs

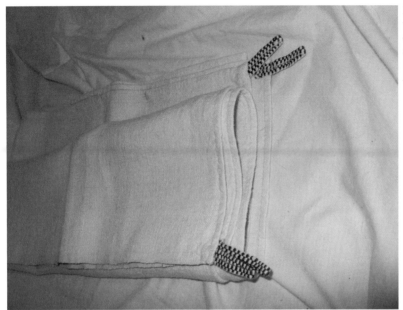

Bleached linen towel with handwoven linen checkerboard tabs, hand sewn to corners. *Collection of Eleanor Bittle, The Tape Lady ©.*

Tabs on "Show" Towels

Decorated hand towels, or "show" towels, with their long embroidered panels of linen, held great importance for the Pennsylvania German community. Almost completely the work of the adolescent girls, they were intended for the display of the young woman's needlework skills in colorful embroidery work, with an eye toward attracting a husband. A decorated towel hung on the *Schtubb* ("stove" in Pennsylvania German) room or sitting room side of the door, for family and guests to see and admire. Their height of popularity was between 1820 and 1850.[22] Each show towel had a tab sewn on each upper corner, for the hanging of the towel. These hanging tabs could either be store-bought or homemade. There seem to have been more commercially made cotton twill tabs than handwoven. The handloomed tabs typically were of linen, in natural, bleached white, and brown. Cotton handwoven tapes generally were in blue, red, white, and blue, or multicolors. "As with the weaving of their tape, 'towel makers made loops however they could, with whatever materials were at hand," states Ellen Gehret.[23]

Jerry Yanchek and daughter, Emily Voelker, reenacting the hand sewing of decorated "show" towels during the Goschenhoppen Festival, Green Lane, Pennsylvania, in 2009. Notice women's linen cap tape ties and red cotton embroidery thread on towels.

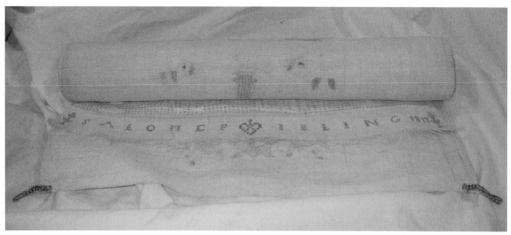

Decorated handspun and -woven linen "show" towel, with embroidery, dated 1817. Handwoven linen tape tabs of bleached linen, brown and indigo blue, hand sewn to corners. Purchased at York, Pennsylvania, auction by Eleanor Bittle. Notice a bit of "drawn work" above embroidered lettering. *Collection of Eleanor Bittle, The Tape Lady ©.*

Close-up of one of the handwoven linen tape tabs. Red cotton embroidery thread can be clearly seen. *Collection of Eleanor Bittle, The Tape Lady ©.*

The "Tape" Measure

In the past, seamstresses used to make their own tape measures. A commercial length of ribbon would be marked in ink or be embroidered, using an ell measurement that was equal to 1¼ yards.[24]

—Marion Channing,
The Textile Tools of Colonial Homes

Tape measures from two different eras. Top is modern plastic (ugh!) tape measure; bottom is commercially woven cotton twill tape measure with stamped measurements.

Tape for Agricultural Uses
Feed, Seed, and Grain Bags

Tape was sewn to the corners of the grain or seed bags to tie the bags closed, and as a loop for hanging. Authorities now realize that the two bast fibers, hemp and linen, were used interchangeably, wherever appropriate. This would apply to the woven bag, as well as to the tape. The farm families used whatever fiber was on hand. "Grain bags have been seen that have been in constant and hard use for seventy years, homespun from coarse flax and hemp. I have several bags about four feet long and 2 feet wide. They have the date of their manufacture, 1789, and the initials of the weaver, and have linen tapes woven in at each side."[25] (See more in Chapter 4, Historical Tape Pattern Directory.)

Corners of two handwoven tow grain bags. The grain bag on right has handwoven tow tape hand sewn to its corner. (See Chapter 4 for other examples of grain bags with tape attached.) *Collection of Eleanor Bittle, The Tape Lady ©.*

Other Agricultural Uses

Tape was also used in a myriad of other ways, such as tape tabs for tool handles, animal leads made of tape, and powder horn or hunting straps.

Chair Tape at the Hancock Shaker Village

The height of making chair tape in the Shaker communities of New York and New England was during the mid nineteenth century. The tape was, at first, specifically woven for their personal chair making. There were two different models of tape looms used, the tabletop or the standing, floor model. By 1870, though, the communities were selling their tape commercially. It was woven in their factory. There were two average sizes of tape available: one-inch-wide and half-inch-wide, all woven from their own processed wool. [26]

Textiles in the Industrial Age

For many hundreds of years, the making of hand-woven textiles had historically been an extremely laborious process. Textile production, one of the first to be industrialized, changed many aspects of life for many people, in many countries. Around 1760, the Industrial Revolution began in England, with other countries following soon after. Dramatic changes took place economically, as well as socially, with the replacement of hand production by massive mechanization. During the beginning of the nineteenth century, this formidable struggle between hand and power machinery began to really take shape. Individual workers had become part of the machine operation by 1850, losing their identities, becoming nothing more than textile mill slaves.

Mass-produced, commercially milled threads and textiles were much quicker to produce, and so much cheaper to purchase, at the expense of the workers who made it all possible.

By 1850, tape was commercially woven in US mills. Twill tape became the common mass-produced commercial ribbon. During the 1860s, rubber thread was woven into bands of tape and called elastic tape, which was commercially woven in the United States. This would lead to socks with elastic bands around the tops. No more need for garters! Handwoven tape continued to be woven, though, probably by older women, until

the early twentieth century. In his book *Mennonite Arts,* Clarke Hess includes a photo of several bundles of handwoven tape, dated circa 1850–1875, woven by a Mennonite family in Lancaster County, Pennsylvania.[27] In her personal tape collection, Eleanor Bittle has a bundle of tape dated circa 1927.

Commercially Woven "Red Tape," Then and Now

The story of where the term "red tape" comes from has always been hazy. The following is one proposed theory. There is no thoroughly documented historical origin, but some researchers think that it began during the 1516 to 1556 Spanish administration of King Charles V. During the sixteenth to seventeenth centuries, the British and the Spanish government administrations began writing their legal documents on parchment. After being rolled into scrolls, certain documents were tied with commercially woven tape, specifically dyed red. The red tape wrapped around the most important documents would alert officials that those documents needed attention before others. This practice was quickly copied by many other European monarchs, to ease the growing load of bureaucratic backlogs.[28]

This was the beginning of the infamous "red tape," the rules and decrees that plague excessive bureaucracies around the world, even today. Wrapped in tape that was dyed red, the legal documents would definitely stand out from other documents, symbolizing their importance. Safflower, a source of red dye for many hundreds of years, was used until the twentieth century to dye the tapes for securing government and legal documents in the British Empire.[29]

There are a number of novels that include the term "red tape." They include The Scarlet Letter (1850) by Nathaniel Hawthorne, and David Copperfield (1917) by Charles Dickens.

At some time in modern history, the British changed the color of their legal tape from red to pink. The legal profession there still wraps their briefs, the official documents outlining a case, in tape, though now they are tied in leather or cardboard file cases.

At many law offices, in many countries, commercially woven pink or red tape continues to be wrapped around legal folders and documents, a tradition still in use from long ago.

Swirl of commercially woven cotton tape, dyed red, by Wayne Mills, Philadelphia, Pennsylvania.

On left, Mary Jane Myers, Quality Administrator, checking warp-faced polyester tape, from giant spools to finished tape, at Wayne Mills Company.

Wayne Mills Commercial Tape

Commercial tape, with its many uses in today's world, remains important. To give you an overview of this aspect of tape, I took a tour of Wayne Mills Company in Philadelphia, Pennsylvania. The company is a good example of how textile mills have evolved into clean and safe environments for their workers. Mary Jane Myers, Quality Administrator, who has worked there since 1991, described the history of their textile mill and gave me a full explanation of their weaving looms; their processes, including dyeing and bleaching; and the finished woven products they sell.

Wayne Mills Company has been an operating textile tape mill for 104 years, founded in 1910. For all of these years, they have been manufacturing a variety of narrow fabrics, called "tape." A key to their success has been their willingness to adapt to the changing needs for tape, from decade to decade. Commercially woven tape is still very much used in our modern world and Wayne Mills Company is there to meet the challenge. Mary Jane told me that their business plan has been very productive. By having a lot of square footage in their mill, they are able to keep a large raw inventory and the business can give customers a quick turnaround, three to four weeks, where most manufacturers need six to eight weeks in production. During my visit, I observed an Amish crew, from Lancaster County, Pennsylvania—my hometown!—building an additional storage building for their expanding needs.

Cones of yarn, ready to be put on warp to be woven into tape products, at Wayne Mills Company.

Another key to their success is the fact that Wayne Mills Company is a family operation, spanning six generations. The founding brothers, William and Arthur Milnes, began their operation at Wayne Junction, on the south side of Wayne Avenue in the Germantown section of Philadelphia. When Wayne Mills Company was incorporated, in 1910, they were weaving narrow fabrics that were high volume/low profit items. John Milnes joined his brothers a few years later and the ownership and managing of the company was transferred to his family. He is the great-grandfather of Laura Diamond, the treasurer of Wayne Mills Company. From 1942 to 1948 they moved the operation in stages to the present site, a former carpet mill, and then were able to buy the property in 1976.

Wayne Mills Company has quite a history of adapting to the market's changing needs, from weaving zipper twill tape, to serving the apparel industry with skirt and collar straps, and later, weaving medical and hospital gown tape ties and bicycle handlebar tape. At one point in their

Warp yarn ready to be woven into tape products, at Wayne Mills Company.

Large bundles of dyed woven tape, ready to be taken out of skeins to process for shipment to customer. Bundles are so much larger than bundles of handwoven tape! Notice bundles are tied with cotton tape, ever functional, at Wayne Mills Company.

history, they actually wove the straps on the animal cracker boxes that many of us grew up with.

Walking through the aisles, I was shown large bins of mop tape, safety tape, black awning tape for RVs, grosgrain ribbon, carpet binding tape, and the edging tape that holds up American flags on the flagpole. They can even put flame retardant on a customer's tape order. Not much upholstery trimming is manufactured at Wayne Mills Company, though. Other mills produce large volumes of that type of trim. The woven yarn used for their tape is mainly cotton and polyester. Needless to say, I was very impressed by it all. Mary Jane told me that Wayne Mills Company produces up to 1.5 million yards of tape every week. When I think of my little box tape loom and the amount of tape that I'm capable of weaving in a week—*wow!*

I was especially interested in their production of "red tape," in relation to the history of "cutting through the red tape" in legal documents. Mary Jane explained to me that Wayne Mills Company has been weaving this (balanced) plain weave pattern, sold as "red tape," since its beginning.

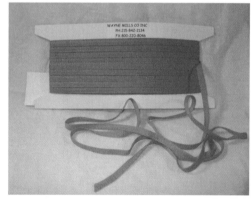

Wayne Mills Company red tape in tape holder.

This material is woven with natural cotton yarn and then dyed to the customers' standard. It is always ¼" wide. In 2013, Wayne Mills Company wove 100,000 yards of red tape, with some of it to be used in courthouses and law offices to bind official documents.

Over the years, they have upgraded to more automated looms and high-speed machinery. In

Needle looms. Warp yarn in background and woven tape shown in front, at Wayne Mills Company.

Mill worker Noi Senouthai holding up bundle of woven tape, ready for dyeing process, at Wayne Mills Company.

1987, needle looms were introduced for their increased speed and better quality control. Shuttle looms were phased out by 2001. Over the years, this change has brought down the workforce from 200 employees to 65. I had the opportunity to chat with several of the workers, who had been employed at the mill for many years. They told me that there isn't much turnover; it's mostly longtime workers there, who are quite satisfied with their jobs. Mary Jane told me how proud they are that management is open to new ideas from all employees in the mill to help make the processes run more smoothly.

By working together and changing with the times, the Wayne Mills Company family and employees of this commercial tape mill have kept their historical and economic relevance in today's market.[30]

2. Tape Looms and Tape Loom Makers

Colonial Tape Looms

A tape loom was a common piece of furniture in the homes of many of the settlers in early America. Made of wood, these looms were relatively lightweight and portable for weaving in different spots in the home or even outside, where there might be better light. Because of their frequent use, they also had to be sturdy, to last for a number of years.

The loom could have been built by a local woodworker or bought in the village store. Because of its simple form, though, there was a good chance that a family member, probably a husband or a father, would have built the family tape loom. Being a very personal item in the home, this functional little loom was sometimes embellished according to the family wishes. Traditional decorations for family looms included a variety of hand carvings, heart or tulip shapes, painting, grain work, staining, or marbling. A tape loom could have been built as a gift for a relative or a friend, so it might be decorated in a personal manner, with the date and initials of the maker or recipient inscribed on the rigid heddle. It is possible that it was the farmwife who had the last say as to the style, size, and design of the family tape loom, since she, as well as the children and grandparents, would have been weaving their family tape.

The Romantic Loom? *Tape Tale #2*

We had a hearty stew for supper, cooked on the open hearth. The Dutch oven was hung on the crane away from the hot wood coals, for the stew to slowly simmer. The spider pan had fried up some nice veggies to go with the stew. It was well worth the wait.

After our quiet meal, my husband surprised me with a box tape loom, for our second wedding anniversary. It really was a nice functional loom, decorated with a large tulip painted on the top of the rigid heddle. He even hand carved my name into the curly maple wood, along with today's date, March 12, 1794. Just like wedding anniversaries 200 years later, where the husband presents his wife with yet another kitchen appliance—wonderfully functional gifts, but not all that romantic. But my new tape loom would be passed down in the family, for many others to use, which meant it tied us to the future of our family.

Wooden box tape loom with interesting design. Notice jagged wooden diagonal bar on far right. The saying "What they had, they used" describes the making of some of the tape looms of the region. *Collection of Landis Valley Village and Farm Museum, Pennsylvania Historical and Museum Commission.*

Because of such a variety of personal choices and appearances, when a collector comes across a historical tape loom, it could be shaped and embellished completely differently from another of similar provenance. They were built as "one of a kind," not mass produced. Today, this makes a loom discovery that much more exciting! But it is important to remember that they all work relatively the same way, to make strong and functional tape.

"Father Helped Me"

A delightful novel for young readers by Lucille Long, called *Anna Elizabeth*, is set in 1748, and is an account of a Dunkard maid (Dunkards were a Plain religious sect) who lived in the Oley region, northwest of Philadelphia, Pennsylvania. It describes Anna receiving, for her birthday, "a handloom which [her brother] had made almost entirely by himself. 'Father helped me burn the holes in it,' he said."[1]

He would have been referring to the rigid heddle holes that the warp threads would pass through, during the warping process and weaving.

Simple wooden box tape loom with rigid heddle nailed to front. *Collection of Landis Valley Village and Farm Museum, Pennsylvania Historical and Museum Commission.*

Tape loom by John Drissell, 1795, Lower Milford Township, Pennsylvania. White pine, red oak, paint. *Courtesy of Winterthur Museum. Gift of Henry Francis du Pont.*

Wooden Canadian box tape loom, painted white. *Collection of Eleanor Bittle, The Tape Lady ©.*

Simple wooden box tape loom with narrow rigid heddle and large reel in back. *Collection of Landis Valley Village and Farm Museum, Pennsylvania Historical and Museum Commission.*

Larger view of the simple wooden box tape loom shown on page 46; rigid heddle nailed to front. *Collection of Landis Valley Village and Farm Museum, Pennsylvania Historical and Museum Commission.*

Tape loom by John Drissell, 1795, Lower Milford Township, Pennsylvania. White pine, oak, walnut, paint. *Courtesy of Winterthur Museum. Bequest of Henry Francis du Pont.*

Three Different Tape Loom Models

"These tape-looms are a truly ancient form of appliance for the hand-weaving of narrow bands, a heddle-frame. They were rudely primitive in shape, but served well the colonists in all our original states."[2] As the Pennsylvania Germans would say, "Function first and then a little pretty."

There are three different models and sizes of tape looms:

- The paddle loom, sometimes referred to as the "knee" or "lap" loom.
- The box loom.
- The floor loom, or "standing" loom.

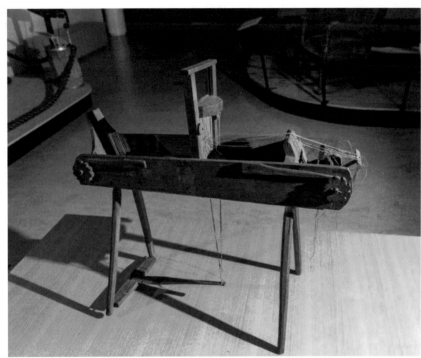

Floor Loom: Floor, standing, tape loom. Front and back ratchet system and back reel. Only one foot treadle, and unusual pulley system for rigid heddle. Linen tape being woven on loom. *Collection of Schwenkfelder Library and Heritage Center.*

Paddle Loom: Wooden paddle, or knee, tape loom, dated 1695, not documented. Linen tape, hand woven by Eleanor Bittle. *Collection of Eleanor Bittle, The Tape Lady ©.*

Box Loom: Wooden box tape loom. It doesn't get much simpler than that! Peg in back for brake. Linen tape, hand woven by Eleanor Bittle, with fish netter as shuttle. *Collection of Eleanor Bittle, The Tape Lady ©.*

Wooden box loom with large back reel inside small box. This little box loom has all parts necessary for weaving tape. The ratchet brake is hidden inside. *Courtesy of Gay McGeary.*

Each has its own distinct characteristics, so one loom might be favored over the others by a weaver, for different reasons. See Chapter 5 for an in-depth explanation of each of these models of looms. There are also other tape loom designs that originated in other cultures, for example, the Scandinavian band looms that are described at the end of this chapter.

All three models of tape looms have important parts that make the looms functional:

- The **rigid heddle**. All three models of tape looms have a rigid heddle, with slots and holes, to change the warp shed.

In addition, the box and the floor looms need the following:

- The **back beam**. This part allows the warp threads to be wound onto the back and stored before weaving. There are two styles, the **reel** and the **roller**.
- The **ratchet brake system**. This important part tightens and loosens the tension in the warp threads as the weaving proceeds.

The Paddle Tape Loom

The paddle, knee, or lap tape loom is the simplest of the three models. Consisting of only one flat piece of wood, it measures, on average, ½" thick by 8" wide by 20" high. This loom, which is basically a simple rigid heddle, is quite easy to make. It is the quickest to warp, and the most portable of all the looms. Since it is completely flat, it fits nicely in a suitcase and packs well for traveling.

The shape of the loom is quite functional, with the concave area below the rigid heddle being propped between the weaver's legs. The warp threads run through the holes and slots. The knotted warp threads behind the rigid heddle are simply tied to a pole or post. The front warp threads are tied together in an overhand knot and usually held in the weaver's hand. By moving the warp threads up and down, the two sheds are formed.

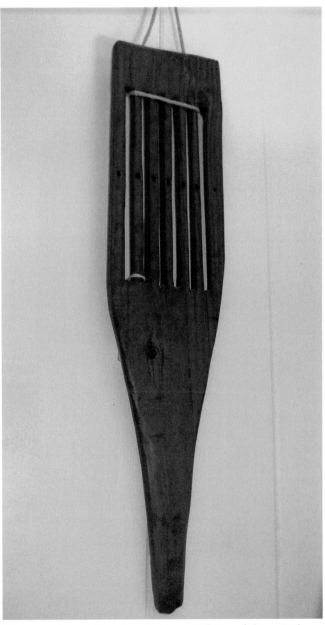

Narrow, wooden paddle, or knee, tape loom. *Collection of Eleanor Bittle, The Tape Lady* ©.

Wooden paddle, or knee, tape loom, hanging upside down for convenient storage. Hand woven linen tape in "check" pattern by Eleanor Bittle, using her fish netter as shuttle. *Collection of Eleanor Bittle, The Tape Lady* ©.

Wall of wooden paddle tape looms from Eleanor Bittle's extensive collection. These knee looms, as she prefers to call them, all have the same basic design, but notice the variety in overall sizes and shapes of different looms. Two looms in top left corner are both upside down, for convenient storage. All have linen tape, woven by Eleanor Bittle. *Collection of Eleanor Bittle, The Tape Lady* ©.

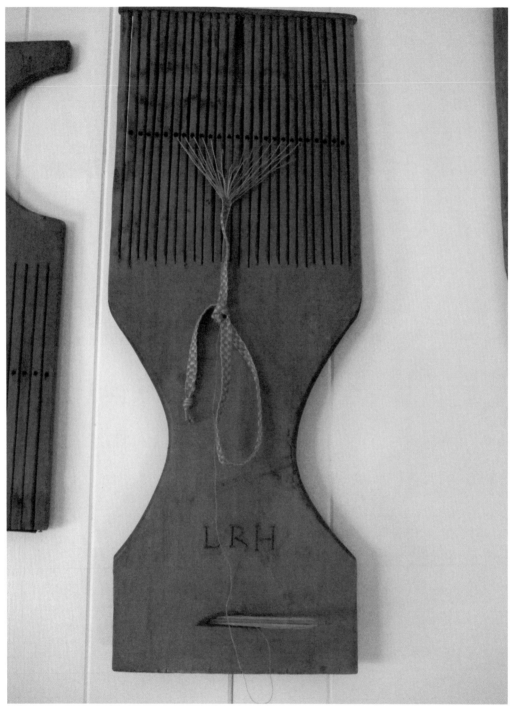

Wooden paddle, or knee, tape loom, with linen "check" tape, hand woven by Eleanor Bittle. Fish netter as shuttle attached. Initials "LRH" inscribed in the wood. *Collection of Eleanor Bittle, The Tape Lady* ©.

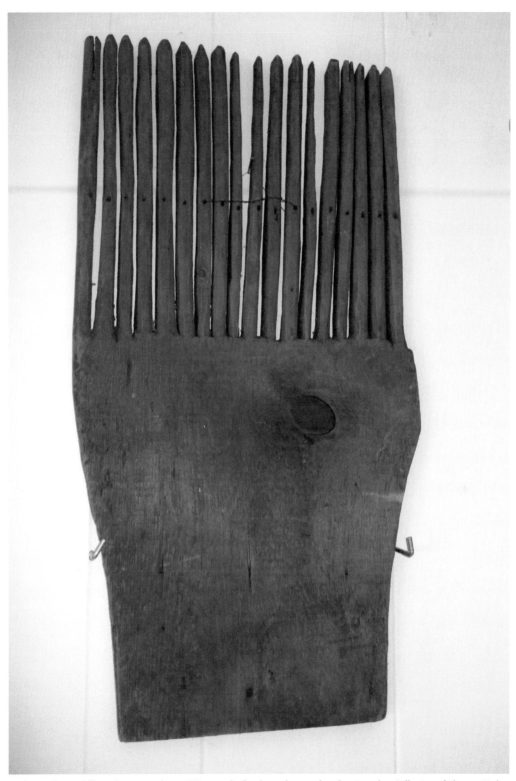

Wide wooden paddle, or knee, tape loom. Wire attached to keep the wooden slats in order. *Collection of Eleanor Bittle, The Tape Lady* ©.

Parts of the Paddle Loom

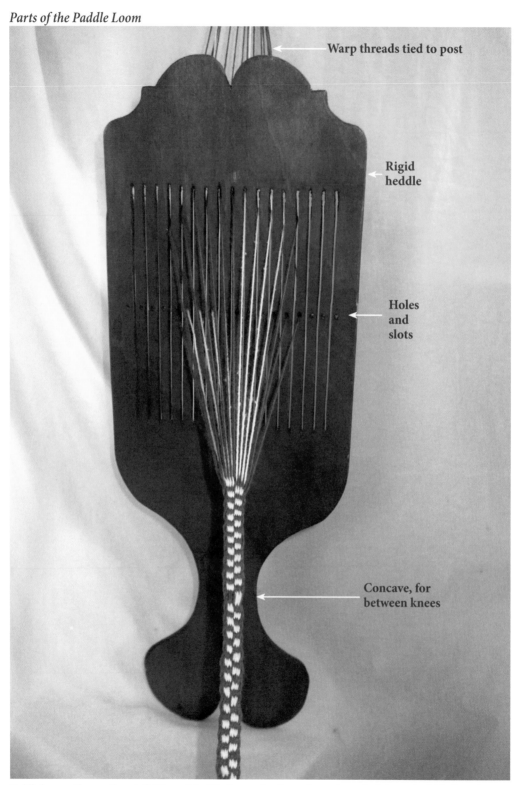

Warp threads tied to post

Rigid
heddle

Holes
and
slots

Concave, for
between knees

Paddle loom with warp threads fed through heddle for weaving. Loom is constructed of plywood, which shows how simply this loom can be made. Tape woven by student.

The Floor Paddle Tape Loom

This is very similar to the standard paddle loom that is propped between the weaver's legs. But in this case, the paddle is extended into a much longer length, to the floor. No need to prop it up between the knees. The rigid heddle is chair height and more comfortable for the weaver. There is a flat piece of wood attached on the floor for the weaver's feet to set on, giving the loom more stability. As with the standard paddle loom, the warp threads are tied to a post behind and held in the weaver's hand in the front.

Wooden floor paddle loom, bought at flea market in Lancaster, Pennsylvania, for two dollars, many years ago. Seller had no idea of its use. Missing far right end of rigid heddle and top wooden cap for heddle, but it weaves well and makes good tape. *Collection of author.*

The Box Tape Loom

There are quite a number of original box tape looms that are still in good condition and are functional, after all these many years. They may be quite pricey these days if discovered at an antique shop or through an auction house. Traditionally made box looms varied a great deal, in size and decoration. Even the functional loom parts may be somewhat different, depending on who designed the loom. I find these variables to be quite interesting. Rarely do you find two looms exactly alike. The box loom is usually an open wooden box, with a few additional parts to it. Many box looms range in size from about 9 inches wide by 20 inches long, with a rigid heddle averaging 14 inches high. Traditionally, box loom dimensions varied. Some were built with a lot of fancy work, with very elaborate ornamentation and some are a work of simplicity. As with the paddle loom, the weaver holds the warp bundle in front of the rigid heddle and alternately lowers and raises the warp threads by hand, to make the two sheds.

The Rigid Heddle

In the front of the loom, a rigid heddle stands vertically inside of the box. There may be a narrow drawer in the box front, for holding the shuttle and scissors, or a "tape" measure.

The Back Beams

There are two different types of back beams that are built into the back of box and floor looms. The first type is the **roller.** Some box looms have **two rollers**, one in the front and one in the back. The second type of back beam is the **reel**.

The Roller

This is the simpler type of back beam, where the warp threads are initially tied on and wound around, to store the warp threads while weaving.

Wall of wooden box tape looms of various sizes and shapes. *Collection of Eleanor Bittle, The Tape Lady* ©.

Parts of the Box Tape Loom

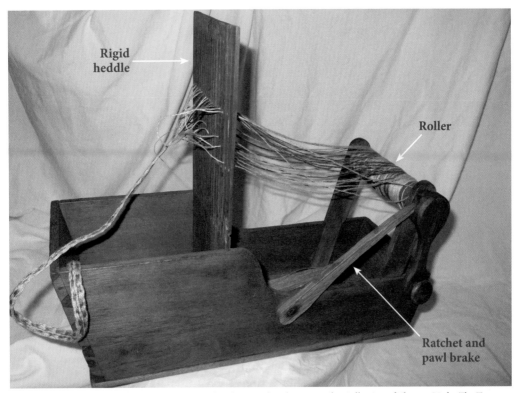

Wooden box tape loom with linen "check" tape, hand woven by Eleanor Bittle. *Collection of Eleanor Bittle, The Tape Lady ©.*

Two Rollers

Some box looms are designed with two rollers, the back roller, as well as a cloth roller (which collects the woven cloth), in the front of the loom. See page 63 for more examples. A small hole in the bottom of the rigid heddle allows the woven tape to slip through, winding it on to the cloth roller with its own ratchet system. The woven tape can be wound on to the cloth roller, keeping it out of the way and orderly, which would be quite practical.

Wooden tape loom with metal staple attached to middle of back roller in box frame. Warp threads can be slid through staple and secured with overhand knot and wound around roller for storage while weaving. *Collection of Landis Valley Village and Farm Museum, Pennsylvania Historical and Museum Commission.*

Reproduction wooden floor tape loom with knob on back roller.
Warp threads can be hooked over knob and wound around roller
for storage while weaving. *Collection of Landis Valley Village and
Farm Museum, Pennsylvania Historical and Museum Commission.*

Wooden back roller sitting in box frame. Notice metal
nail in middle of roller. Warp threads can be hooked over
nail and wound around roller for storage while weaving.
*Collection of Landis Valley Village and Farm Museum,
Pennsylvania Historical and Museum Commission.*

Box tape loom, made of cherry wood, mid-eighteenth century. Notice the slot below rigid heddle that handwoven tape is entering to be wrapped around front beam for storage. *Collection of Daniel Boone Homestead.*

Another manner of collecting woven tape: a notch carved into front roller, allowing woven tape to be collected in another front roller, close to rigid heddle. This feature is similar to design of floor tape looms. Exceptional length in front of loom gives larger weaving area and weaver does not have to hold front warps in hands, under tension. Handwoven cotton tape woven by the author. *Courtesy of Hans Herr House and Museum.*

Wooden box tape loom showing hole in front of rigid heddle for woven tape to go through to front roller, for collecting. *Private collection.*

Wooden box tape loom with hole in rigid heddle for woven tape to pass through and front roller to collect woven tape. Notice back reel for winding on warp threads. *Private collection.*

The Reel

The other, more elaborate type of back beam is the reel. This takes more time for a woodworker to build, but makes winding on the warp threads quicker and easier than the roller.

Wooden box tape loom with exceptionally large reel for winding on warp threads. *Private collection.*

Wooden box tape loom with linen warp wound around the reel. Warping of loom by friend of author. *Private collection.*

The Ratchet Brake System

The last important loom part of the box tape loom is the ratchet brake system, to loosen or tighten the warp tension as the warp threads move through the loom. Looms could have either a simple ratchet and pawl device, or a more complicated setup, made of wood or sometimes metal. They could have a variety of interesting handles to crank the ratchet, as well.

Wooden box tape loom with ratchet and pawl brake on loom. *Private collection.*

The Floor/Standing Tape Loom

The wooden floor tape loom is the most sophisticated of the three models of tape looms. It has more complicated parts and works more like a larger floor loom. This wooden loom is shaped like a narrow table or box, with three or four long legs attached.

It contains two individual wooden rigid heddles, attached to a frame, by leather or rope straps, in the middle of the loom, on a pulley system. The two rigid heddles are tied with rope, leather, or even tape, to the two foot treadles. These two treadles pull each heddle down separately, creating one of the two sheds. There can be either a reel or a roller acting as the back beam.

The floor model can be really appreciated when the weaving begins. With the front warp threads tied to the front of the loom, and the two heddles moving up and down with the treadles, the weaver's hands are free to pass the shuttle back and forth in the sheds. I imagine that most floor tape looms were considered the power horse loom, in that much more tape could be woven, quicker than on the box or paddle looms.

Since the floor tape loom is higher and longer than the box or paddle looms, it does take up more space in a room. This could have been a consideration during colonial times, when living in a small log house, with many children. Also, transporting this larger loom would tend to be more cumbersome.

This wooden floor tape loom had been a working artifact when I wove on it while working at Landis Valley Village and Farm Museum. Used for weaving narrow, one-eighth-inch bleached linen tape for women's linen cap ties. *Collection of Landis Valley Village and Farm Museum, Pennsylvania Historical and Museum Commission.*

Parts of the Tape Floor Loom

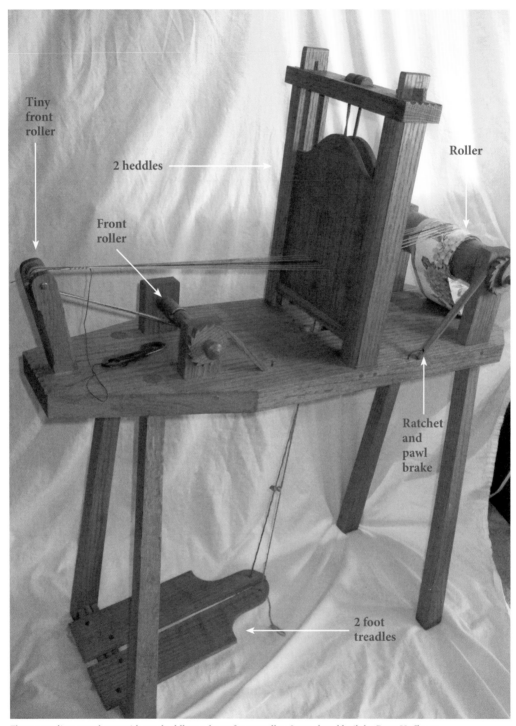

Tiny
front
roller

2 heddles

Roller

Front
roller

Ratchet
and
pawl
brake

2 foot
treadles

Floor, standing, tape loom with two heddles and two foot treadles. Loom hand built by Dave Hoffman.

Cultural Differences in Tape Looms

New England Styles of Tape Looms
The Paddle Tape Loom

It is the general opinion that during the early American settlement period, this very simple loom was more popular in the New England region than in the lower colonies. When asked during an interview, Wendy Christie, a southeastern Pennsylvania collector and antique dealer in historical eighteenth and nineteenth century early American textiles, and Alan Keyser, a local historian and author, they both felt that the paddle loom was not used with frequency in the Pennsylvania German tradition; that it was more of a New England loom.[3] But, that is not to say that other settlers throughout the colonies did not use this loom, as well. As seen earlier in this chapter, Eleanor Bittle has an extensive collection of knee or paddle looms. Weaving in the New England tradition is somewhat different, in that the front knotted warp bundle is tied to the weaver's belt. With the weaver creating the needed tension, the hands are free for throwing the shuttle and weaving.[4]

The Box Tape Loom

The New England style box tape loom had several additional moving parts in their box looms. There were usually two rigid heddles attached to the wooden frame that would move up and down, creating the two sheds. And a special, built-in beater would be situated in front of the set of rigid heddles. It appears to have been designed similarly to a floor or barn loom, only on a much smaller scale.

Wooden box tape loom, typical of New England region. Notice built-in beater and two wire heddles, on small pulley system. *Collection of Gay McGeary.*

The Floor Tape Loom

As with the box tape loom, the New England style floor loom also had a built-in beater, working the same way as the New England box loom style. Other than that addition, this style of floor loom is similar to most floor tape looms, with two heddles and foot treadles to open the two sheds.

The English "Fringe" or "Trim" Loom

This English style box tape loom, sometimes called a "fringe" or "trim" loom, was popular throughout the colonies. The design of this loom, in many instances, was more petite than other box looms and might have a softer, more refined finish to it. A number of them had only 25 holes and slots, so they would be limited in the width of the tape woven. They were a symbol of fashion, used more often by English women as somewhat of a "hobby" loom, for the weaving of fringe and other trims.

Sarah Mifflin's little loom (see page 16) is a wonderful example of a "trim" loom.

Reproduction English box "trim" loom, hand crafted by Jonathan Seidel. Loom modeled after English box loom from Williamsburg Museum collection.

Close-up of English box loom. Number of small compartments in front drawer could have held different colored warp threads for loom's warping process.

The Scandinavian Style of Tape Looms

The Scandinavian cultures are known for their traditional tape weaving, called Nordic Baltic bands, Balkan bands, or simply band weaving. Their cultures remain alive with their traditional costumes, including the handwoven bands, worn for celebrating their native festivals. Different styles of rigid heddles and box band looms have been used for many centuries and traditionally are quite ornately carved wooden band looms.

Their rigid heddle looms are small, flat looms, sometimes referred to as "floating" or "gate" looms.

The heddle literally floats in the middle of the warp threads that are tied to the weaver's belt and a post behind the heddle. The sheds are formed by pulling on the top handle, up or down, as the weaving takes place.

There are also double-holed gate or floating looms, which have an extra set of holes in the heddle to weave their famous "pick-up" patterning. The photo on page 72 has an interesting set of extra "slots."

Scandinavian rigid heddle loom. *Collection of Susan Sharpless Messimer.*

Scandinavian rigid heddle loom. *Private collection.*

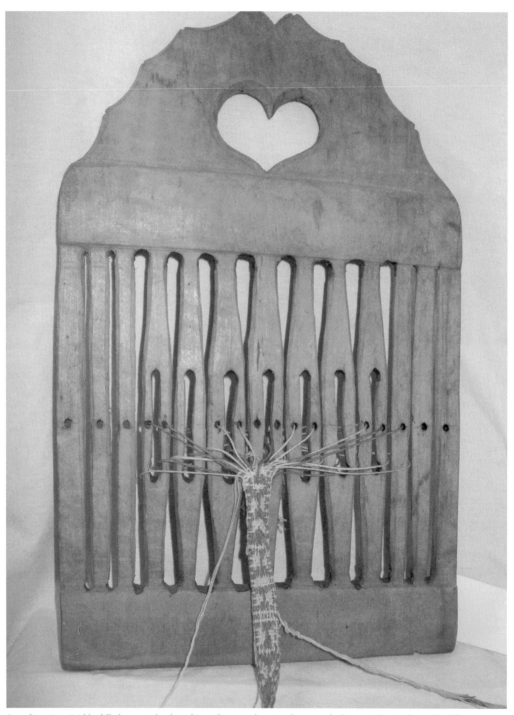

Scandinavian rigid heddle loom with a bit of Scandinavian linen pick-up work shown in front of rigid heddle. *Collection of author.*

Box band looms are similar to typical box tape looms, with either a single-holed heddle or a double-holed heddle. As with the "gate" loom that has a double-holed heddle, this style of box loom is used for weaving the pick-up technique into their bands. Beautiful patterns can be created, with raised designs lying on top of the background band.

Double-holed heddle box tape looms have been found in southeastern Pennsylvania. Were these looms used for weaving pick-up work or possibly just to make stronger tape, for around the barn? Something to be explored at a later date. The Landis Valley Village and Farm Museum example shown at right has two sets of very large heddle holes, as well as a large hole in the front of the heddle for the finished tape to go through to be stored; possibly for weaving heavy tow flax or hemp into a strong farming tape.

When I mentioned this style of tape loom to Eleanor Bittle, her reaction was, "I've never seen any pick-up in southeastern Pennsylvania. More likely to be Scandinavian."[5] See Appendix 2 for more on Scandinavian tape looms.

Double holed box loom, possibly used for weaving thick tow linen or hemp. *Collection of Landis Valley Village and Farm Museum, Pennsylvania Historical and Museum Commission.*

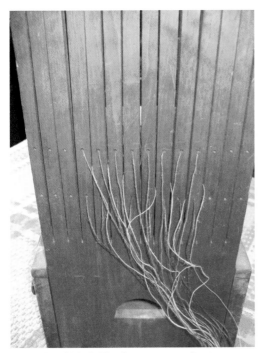

Front of double holed box loom. *Private collection.*

Antique or Reproduction Tape Looms

There are original tape looms that can be found at auctions or flea markets, but they are becoming hard to find. They can also be purchased through Internet auctions, but that can be tricky, since you cannot actually examine the loom. Make sure you can determine that the loom has all of its parts and is functional for your needs.

Sometimes "historical" is not too practical for our modern fibers. I had a student in one of my tape weaving classes who was excited to have found a simple box loom for sale at an antique shop. She brought it to the class, frustrated with the holes in the rigid heddle. This was a beautiful antique loom, but the holes were so tiny, built for very fine handspun linen from long ago. The student learned that she could use the loom only with very thin warp threads to go through the holes. She decided to also purchase a reproduction box tape loom, with larger heddle holes, to give her more choices in warp threads.

Floating rigid heddles can be purchased commercially and used in the same manner as the Scandinavian "floating" band loom, tying the front warp bundle to the weaver's belt. Another style allows the floating heddle to be placed inside

Reproduction floating heddle loom inside of wooden frame. Loom was hand crafted by Jonathan Seidel. Note: Loom frame can also be used for card weaving.

of a wooden frame with front and back beams and ratchet brake systems for winding on the warp threads.

Tape Loom Makers

If you want a traditional, reproduction tape loom, you can find them for purchase at some certain museum stores, or you can find a loom that's been hand crafted by a woodworker. Caution is needed when considering the purchase of a reproduction loom.

The first reproduction tape loom that I bought was a pretty little wooden box loom, which I found sitting in the window of a museum store. It was painted green, with a marbled effect. It looked like a simple, easy-to-use box loom. What could possibly be wrong with it? Once it was home in my studio and I began warping it, I soon realized there was a problem. Because of the "lovely" green paint, I had difficulty getting the warp threads into the slots of the rigid heddle. There was such a buildup of paint seeping into the inside edges of the slots, they were somewhat clogged. Just for pretty! Finally, after much sanding in between the slots, I managed to get much of the excess paint off. But, now there were sanding

Basic reproduction box tape loom built by woodworker at Landis Valley Village and Farm Museum. Notice front and back rollers each have hole for warp threads to go through. Warp threads, tied into overhand knots, fit into carved areas of holes and lie flush against roller, alleviating any bulge. Open handle at top, for carrying.

marks all over the pretty paint on the heddle, and the slots were still quite rough inside. This tape box loom is now more useful as a flowerpot than a tape loom. A lesson learned!

One day, while working in the textile barn at Landis Valley Village and Farm Museum, I was approached by a local woodworker who wanted

Floor or standing reproduction tape loom, hand built by Eric Weit. Instead of two rigid heddles, there are two sets of string heddles. Notice the "helping hands" on the top, or castle, of frame.

Simple box tape loom made of cardboard, with plastic rigid heddle, sold as a kit, by Eleanor Bittle, The Tape Lady.

to make a simple box tape loom to sell in the museum store. He asked if I might help design one, from a weaver's perspective.

I appreciated this approach, since the loom has to be functional to make good tape. The project was enjoyable and went well. I bought one of his looms and have been using it for my own tape weaving for a number of years, as well as the tape weaving classes that I teach.

These stories demonstrate how important it is for a woodworker, whether a professional craftsperson or a family member, to have an understanding of the weaving process before making a loom. When I teach tape weaving workshops, I encourage my students to bring a tape loom to use in the class, so I see an interesting variety of these looms. Most are functional. But others can be a little quirky and take some maneuvering to get them to work well. When finding a tape loom to buy or when having one built, it's a good idea to really examine it, to make sure that the tape weaving experience will be a good one.

Eleanor Bittle has a sturdy cardboard box tape loom for sale. It consists of a kit, with directions for putting the loom together. This is a wonderful loom for children to learn about tape weaving and an inexpensive loom of their own. Her contact information is in Appendix 2.

Visit Warp Seed Studio's Facebook page for information on ordering the box tape loom I've designed.

Jonathan Seidel, Tape Loom Maker

Here's one story of a talented craftsman and his tape loom business.

Jonathan Seidel, from Royersford, Pennsylvania, outside Philadelphia, would admit that these days he is working just as hard, if not harder, in his retirement. In his home basement, he builds tape looms—box, paddle and floor models, as well as custom shuttles.

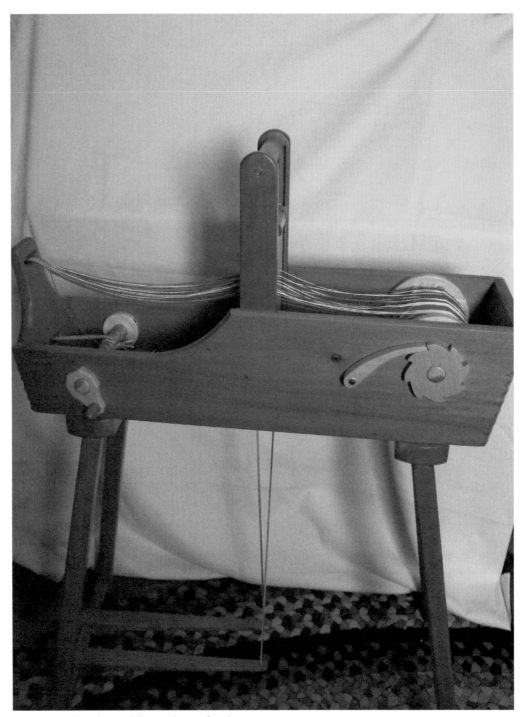

Larger view of Jonathan Seidel's reproduction floor loom.

Miniature reproduction box tape loom, complete with front drawer, hand crafted by Jonathan Seidel. His fine woodworking abilities stand out in this tiny, but functional, working tape loom.

Another of Jonathan Seidel's unique tape loom designs. Modeled after his cat, Shuttle, who appears quite curious about his new friend.

While growing up on a farm, as a boy he made his own toys. He spent forty-five years as a woodworker, making canoes, woodcarvings, and home furnishings.

In 2000 he began making his tape looms to sell, and hasn't stopped since. Jonathan uses a variety of hardwoods. Whether the loom is crafted out of Pennsylvania birdseye or curly maple, cherry, walnut, sycamore, oak, or sassafras, the finished loom feels like silk. Jonathan believes that the sanding down of the wood is very important, but it is also very time consuming. He has an understanding of the weaver's perspective, since his wife, Debbie, is a longtime rug weaver. Jonathan told me, "Light colored wood makes good contrast with warp threads. You can see them better." A weaver would appreciate that kind of detailed thought going into the making of their tape loom.

His most popular model of tape loom is his "three-fourth" size loom. It is 12" long, 11" high,

and 7" wide. This is one of his smallest and most portable looms, with the rigid heddle being removable for transporting. It has 33 slots and holes and the back of each tape loom has a hole to tie the loom to a table, for added warp tension, if needed.

Jonathan is currently crafting some of his tape looms with double holes in the rigid heddle. This gives the weaver the option of weaving in the Scandinavian pick-up manner, if he or she wishes.

This skilled craftsman can make a loom in a couple of weeks. He has worked with customers to reproduce period and custom style looms. His tape looms have homes in the United States, Canada, Germany, Italy, France, and New Zealand, to name a few countries. To date, he has handcrafted approximately 350 tape looms.[6]

Jonathan can be contacted to discuss his tape looms; see Appendix 2.

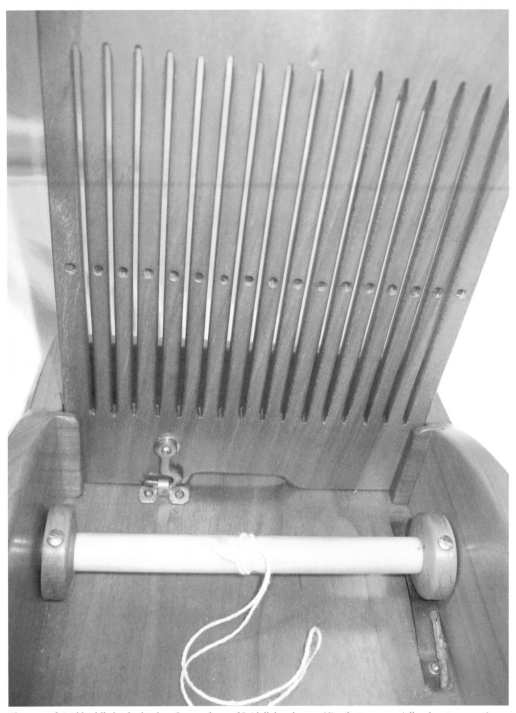

Close-up of rigid heddle latched to box frame of one of Seidel's box looms. Nice feature, especially when transporting loom.

One of Seidel's double-holed heddle box tape looms. Two bundles of reproduced tape on side, hand woven by Dee Lande.

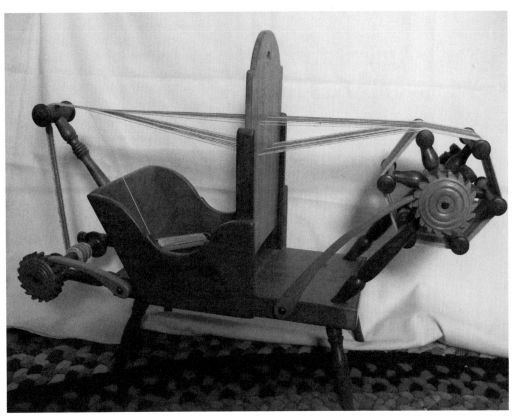

Reproduction tape box loom, hand built by Jonathan Seidel, replica of intricate box tape loom collected by Winterthur Museum (see photo on page 16).

3. Early American Yarns and Dyes for Weaving Tape

This chapter is a short overview of the traditional yarns and dyes used during the early American days. You can consider putting this information to use when working on your tape loom today. There are many books available that are dedicated to a thorough exploration of early American handspun yarn and dyes, including interesting dye recipes for replication.

Early American Yarns

In Europe, before the eighteenth and nineteenth century migrations to America, flax and wool were the predominant fibers used for family cloth needs. When coming to America, people brought with them these fibers that they were familiar with. Early American households used flax, hemp, and sheep's wool in the making of their homespun clothing, as well as all of their other cloth needs, including tape. Self-sufficient, the farmers up and down the coast used these fibers on their family farms. Depending on the climate and location, many farmers would have a flax patch and a hemp patch, along with a flock of sheep for their family's woolen needs.[1]

Once the different fibers were processed, women and girls on the farms were responsible for the spinning of the yarn. The flax was spun

---

Friendly Tape   *Tape Tale #3*

In the spring, our family "pulled" a good crop of flax in the field. That means, if the dew-retted flax doesn't get moldy, we should have an abundant amount to spin this year, 1796. Lots of linen for our family cloth, as well as all of our family tape needs. With our neighbor's wife on the farm up the road being so sick over the past winter, my daughters and I will be spinning a little extra flax into linen, and maybe weaving a little more tape, to share with their family.

---

on the flax wheel, with the flax changing its name to "linen" once spun into thread. The wool was spun on the wool wheel.[2] I imagine this was a peaceful but endlessly necessary chore for the farm wife and her daughters. The finely spun yarn would be plied and wrapped into skeins, ready to be dyed and then woven into a variety of cloth needed by the entire family. Most of the colonial tape was handwoven from linen, hemp, wool, or cotton.

Flax to Linen

The most common fiber raised in this period was flax. Called a bast fiber for its long, fibrous stem, it can grow to 3½ feet tall. Flax underwent an extremely lengthy process in order to spin it into linen thread. Harvesting involved the "pulling season," where members of the farm family would spend time in the field, pulling the flax out of the ground, including the roots, and tying it into standing-up bundles for drying in the field. After the retting stage (explained in the linen dye section), numerous tools and processes were needed to prepare the flax for spinning. These included breaking apart the stems with the flax break, scutching or scraping the fibers, and then heckling to take the remaining short fibers from the long, lustrous fibers.[3] After these many months of preparation, the flax was spun into linen thread by the womenfolk of the family. From weaving fine linen to the thicker, coarser tow, there were many uses for this strong cloth throughout the colonial period. The majority of the family tape was woven from the handspun linen.

Different authorities have their own ideas regarding the ply of the linen thread for traditional tape weaving. In *Rural Pennsylvania Clothing*, Ellen Gehret states that "usually single-ply linen was used for warp and weft."[4] The Historical Tape Pattern Directory (see Chapter 4) consists primarily of 2-ply warp and weft, with several even 3-ply or 4-ply. But, the handspun is very fine, sometimes as thin as sewing thread!

After so many centuries of linen being the most important fiber in cloth making, the first quarter of the nineteenth century saw linen falling away to the rise of cotton and wool production. Many Pennsylvania Germans continued to raise their flax crop and spin it into linen thread, since this was their longstanding tradition. It has been cating the time needed for the handweaving process. As with the continued raising of flax, in southeastern Pennsylvania tape was woven by hand for a much longer period of time. There are accounts of tape being woven into the mid-1800s (as mentioned by Clarke Hess in Chapter 2 of his *Mennonite Arts*) and a little later, as well.

Hemp

Hemp is another bast fiber, similar to flax, but it is capable of growing up to eight feet tall in the field, lending itself to a very long, strong thread once processed. In early America, due to its strength, hemp was used for numerous items, both domestically and commercially. Some examples of its uses were for homespun clothing, paper, rope, grain and feedbags, canvas such as for the Conestoga wagon covers of Lancaster County, Pennsylvania, and ship sails. These are just a small sampling of the many ways that people used hemp in early America.

Being stronger than flax linen, due to its fiber length, hemp can be spun into a fine thread, or a much thicker thread, such as tow. (The myth has been that hemp was only used for thick, coarse threads or rope, used around the barnyard.) If well processed, it can be woven into a thin thread similar to "fine" grade linen. Hemp and flax were sometimes blended, states Les Stark.[9] So there is a good chance that hemp was woven into some of the tape produced on the farms. During my interview with Eleanor Bittle, she commented, "There are reports that tow linen or hemp were used as weft threads in the tape."[10] Since the Pennsylvania Germans were known for using whatever they had on hand, that is definitely possible.

Cotton

In eighteenth-century America, cotton was not as important a fiber as linen. There were serious problems with obtaining the fiber. The seeds had to be picked out by hand, which was extremely tedious. And then there was the matter of where cotton could be grown. The colder climates of the northern colonies did not allow for large quantities to be grown there. Cotton was spun, but on a very limited scale.

Small sample bundle of flax fiber that would be pulled from a field, to be processed into linen thread. Notice seedpods at top, holding flax seeds that can be processed for oils and planting. Bundle is tied with a bit of linen tape, hand woven by author.

recorded that by 1838, when the general changeover to cotton and wool had largely taken place, 700 acres of flax were planted in Berks County, Pennsylvania.[5]

Along with the decline in the flax culture, the growing importance of cotton and wool also led to the decline of handwoven tape. More and more tape was store bought, and with the advent of the Industrial Revolution, it was cheaper than dedi-

Very large handmade rye straw basket, 10.5 inches high by 21 inches in diameter. Lid is not showing. Inside are many flax stricks, bundles of flax that have been processed and are ready for spinning into linen thread on the flax wheel. Basket and contents were bought at a Conestoga Auction Company auction on a York County, Pennsylvania, farmstead in mid-1970s. *Collection of Susan Sharpless Messimer.*

All of this changed with the advent of the cotton gin, invented in 1793 by Eli Whitney. The importance of this simple invention is staggering, allowing cotton cloth production to become the most tremendous change in manufacturing of cloth that ever happened before. Both England and America benefited from this development to the extent that once textile mills were built, homespun and woven fabric plummeted into the background of history. With cotton becoming very cheap to purchase, the flax culture was very much impacted in the lives of the Pennsylvania German farmers. By the 1850s, not much home-spun cotton was around at all.[11]

Tape threads were also changing with the role of cotton expanding in the colonies. Once cotton was commercially spun, cotton could be used to a much larger degree as warp thread, combined with linen or as the weft thread. Because cotton accepted dye much more readily than linen, it allowed for more choices of color, as well.

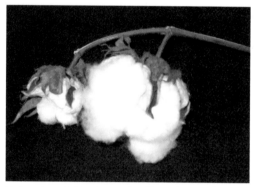

Cotton stem. Cotton is not a fun fiber to harvest. I picked cotton for a month and found it to be extremely laborious work. Notice the long, scratchy stem and the dried pod around the fiber. Gloves are mandatory. Such a little puff of cotton fiber . . . it takes a long time to fill a seventy-pound burlap bag!

Wool

There was handwoven woolen tape, but not as much as linen, hemp, and cotton tape, in south-eastern Pennsylvania. (See page 104 for a wool

Examples of spun and plied hemp, as well as sample of hemp woven with cotton.

tape example.) Wool is not as strong as linen, hemp, or cotton, so it would most likely have been spun and plied tightly before being woven into tape. Wool could have been more commonly used in English "trim" tape, and in other decorative accents, rather than for the strength-requiring tying needs. It does take up dye more easily than linen or hemp does, absorbing the dye color like a sponge, so it lends itself well to colorful accents.

Wool was woven into the tape fringe bound around many of the traditional coverlets, woven of linen or cotton and wool in the nineteenth century. (See page 110 for more information on coverlet tape fringe.) The Scandinavian tape bands have used much more wool for their traditional pick-up pattern work, especially in colorful red wools. See page 70 for a description of this weaving.

Early American Dyes

Linen
Natural Linen
The natural golden-tan or silver-gray colors of linen were predominant throughout the early American colonies. The two colors of natural linen, either a gold or gray tone, depended on the retting process when preparing the flax for spinning. In the New England colonies, people preferred to pond rett their flax, sinking the bundles of flax into ponds and then weighing them down with rocks. This created a long-lasting golden tone to the flax fibers.

Other settlers, such as the Pennsylvania Germans in southeastern Pennsylvania, dew retted their flax. A much more time consuming process, this was the traditional method brought with them from Europe. Many bundles of flax were laid in rows in the field for several weeks, and turned periodically to keep from getting moldy. The morning dew would slowly break down the

The Hub of Hemp Production in Lancaster County, Pennsylvania

Since Lancaster County, Pennsylvania, is my home, I am pleased to include hemp research by Les Stark, author of *Hempstone Heritage I* and his study of early American homespun hemp. There are two local townships, East and West Hempfield Townships, here in Lancaster County, that were named for their hemp production sites back in the eighteenth century. Stark explains, "Mr. Rupp, in his *History of Lancaster County,* said in 1844, on page 189, 'Hempfield Township was so called from the great quantities of hemp raised there.'"[6]

According to Stark, "Between 1681 and 1840, hemp was grown by virtually every farmer in Pennsylvania."[7] With the area's fertile soil, the Pennsylvania Germans developed the reputation for some of the best hemp grown anywhere. Lancaster and York Counties became true hubs of hemp production. Farmers would have their own hemp patches, along with their flax patches. Commercially, hemp became a tremendous cash crop in these regions. Wagons full of hemp went directly to Philadelphia, to be made into strong canvas that would be bought for many sailing rigs along the East Coast. Stark mentions the fact that in order to process such quantities of hemp locally, "between 1720 and 1870, there were over 100 water-powered hemp processing mills in Lancaster County alone."[8] There are still quite a number of local museums in the area that display local hemp millstones, showing the magnitude of the hemp processing operations.

A good-sized hemp millstone, displayed at Hans Herr House and Museum, Willow Street, Pennsylvania. Its conical shape allowed it to be rolled on its side for grinding hemp. Hemp fiber was traditionally used for clothing and rope. *Collection of the Hans Herr House and Museum.*

Several dye plants popular during the early American period: madder root (top); cakes of indigo, and dried black walnut hulls (left).

outside of the stems, making it possible to begin the long preparation process of the fiber for spinning.[12]

Bleached Linen

Being a bast fiber and quite slippery, linen was much harder for dye to adhere to than wool, which sponges up dye color quickly. An alternative to dyeing their linen was to have it bleached, either in the skein or cloth stage. In early America, white symbolized purity and cleanliness. Therefore, the bleaching of the homespun line was very popular. There was more status in having bleached linen instead of the natural, much more common linen. This extra bleaching process was expensive, but implied that one could afford it, hence, status.

According to Eleanor Bittle, either the bleached or natural colored linen would commonly be mixed with one or two contrasting colors. Blues and browns were often seen. Eleanor combines these color choices in much of the linen tape that she reproduces.[13]

The Dyers

There were traditional dyes that were used for the colonial textiles. Along with the much needed dye colors for all of the linen, hemp, cotton, and woolen handspun and woven cloth of this period, the dye would also be needed for the handwoven tape threads, in order to create the contrasting patterns.

Whether in an English, Quaker, or Pennsylvania German community, there were professional dyers, as well as home dyers. Farmwives may have spent a little extra time, if they had it, making their own dye baths for their homespun, using local plants growing around their farmsteads. Or they could have bought dyes at the general store, depending on the expense. Numerous dye manuals were recorded during the colonial period. Many of the manuals were written for the professional dyer's uses, calling for large volumes of textiles and dye materials. Ellen Gehret and Alan Keyser have written that in the Pennsylvania German settlements of southeastern Pennsylvania, during the "homespun period" of early America, professionally dyed materials were more commonly used; sale records of local stores indicate that very little dyeing was done by households. The "blue dyer," who specialized in dyeing with indigo, would dye linen and cotton. Wool would be dyed by the "fuller," the professional wool dyer and finisher.[14]

Handspun wool, hand dyed with indigo by Martha Brunner.

Madder dye being prepared for dyeing session.

Indigo Dye

The colonists favored blue, in all shades, as their most popular color. Handspun linen and indigo blue dye were a perfect match during the colonial period. One of the most important reasons for the popularity of indigo dye was its capacity to adhere to the linen thread. Notice, in the photos in Chapter 4, the large amount of traditional tape with blue linen warp threads, which were dyed with indigo.

During the early American settlements, indigo dye, brought in from the plantations of Jamaica, was available to buy in the village stores or from traveling peddlers. It was packaged in small, compact cakes of pressed powder. Many towns and villages had their own professional "blue" dyers. When working at Landis Valley Village and Farm Museum, I was told that the professional "blue" dyer would have been recognized when walking down the street by his permanently dyed blue hands, from working so long with the indigo dyeing vats. And for all you indigo hand dyers reading this, in a recipe for dying indigo, "One pours fermented human urine over finely pulverized indigo and stands this in the sun."[15] The urine would act as a mordant, keeping in the color. Lovely!

Leftover madder from dyeing process, forming a cake for a future dyeing session.

Red Dyes

Madder Red

The madder dye plant is probably one of the easiest and cheapest dye plants to cultivate and work with. It grows abundantly in southeastern Pennsylvania. The roots containing the beautiful orange-red dye are harvested and dried for the dye pot.

Historically, madder red can be traced back to 3000 BCE, to the time of the Indus civilization.[16] In the colonial days of the eighteenth century, the famous wool "red coats" of the British soldiers

Two skeins of madder dyed wool, drying on tall madder plant.

were dyed with madder. From several different authorities, including Tom Knisely, formerly of The Mannings Handweaving School in East Berlin, Pennsylvania, I have been told that madder red was the Pennsylvania German "red dye of choice," mostly used for the wool that the German settlers homespun and hand wove during the colonial period, as well as for cotton later on. Many of the handwoven coverlets of this period used madder-dyed red wool.

Turkey Red

Another important early American red dye was Turkey red. It delivered a stronger red color than the common madder and was usually prepared by the professional dyers and weavers or sold in local shops. This dye also originated from madder, many years earlier, with the dyers living in the Ottoman Empire, India, and other Eastern countries, like Turkey. The making of this dye was quite complicated and took several months, involving many steps to process. This was not a dye for the home dyer.[17]

It was used mostly on cotton, so once cotton became popular, in the early nineteenth century, Turkey red dye was used more often. Early tapes were woven primarily of linen, a fiber red dye did not adhere to. Therefore, not much red color would have been used in the handwoven tapes of that period. But, again, with the prevalence of cotton as well as Turkey dye, more red cotton warp threads could have been woven into the tapes.

Climbing Madder

I acquired a small quantity of a madder plant from the textile garden at Landis Valley Village and Farm Museum when I worked there. My "madder patch" is still very healthy and has given me a source of red-orange dye, taken from the roots.

When I first planted it, I let it grow as long runners on the ground. But as it continued to spread, I realized it was taking over the garden! Visiting Williamsburg Museum in Virginia, I discovered the benefit of letting it climb up tall, triangular wooden poles. This keeps the madder plant happy and, by growing it vertically, I have more room in the garden for other interesting plants.

Martha Brunner admiring her madder plant growing vertically, and prolifically, in her backyard garden.

Cochineal Red

Another source for obtaining a bold, red dye was cochineal, from the thousands of tiny bugs living on the prickly pear cactus plants of Mexico. Ironically, this strong red dye was discovered in the "New World" by the Spanish conquistadors when invading what is now Mexico, in the 1500s. A valuable treasure for Spain, cochineal was shipped back to Europe, where it became embroiled in political and economic drama.[18] By the colonial period in America, it was quite expensive to buy in stores and was not really used in the southeastern Pennsylvania region.

Brown Dyes

There were quite a number of local plants that produced different shades of brown dyes for the colonists. The leaves and the nut husks of the black walnut trees, native to eastern North America, were popular in the German settlements. They were gathered for dyes in shades of yellows, beiges, and strong or muted browns. A tannin extract of the walnut hulls created the color, but because of the acidic quality of the walnut dye, the color might deteriorate more easily.[19]

Variables in the Dye Process

In early America—and today—a number of variables could influence the final color created from a particular dye bath. This could be frustrating when trying to replicate a particular color for a certain project. The strength and quality of color may vary based upon differences among batches of plant materials, between dyes using fresh or dried plants, and due to growing and harvesting conditions. Also, the dyers' methods, such as the choice of mordant to set the dye, all can play into the reliability of consistency of the dye bath.

I mention these variables because in the Historical Tape Pattern Directory, in Chapter 4, there are several tapes that have very weak color in some of the warp threads. This explanation can be of help in understanding the possible reasons for the faded appearances of the warp threads, other than the fact that the tapes are quite old and may have faded naturally.

4. Handwoven Tape Patterns and Drafts of Early America

Oral Tradition of Tape Patterns

Tape weaving was such an everyday part of life during the early days in rural America, such a common domestic task, that I suspect the writing down of the pattern, in the form of a draft, just didn't seem necessary. People probably wove the same tape patterns their family had been weaving, for many years, without a lot of variation. The passing on of this oral tradition and the repetition of warping and weaving the tape patterns probably began at an early age in a young person's life. During an interview with Eleanor Bittle, "The Tape Lady," I asked for her thoughts on this issue. She strongly confirmed that "No patterns were ever written down."[1]

As documented in the Historical Tape Pattern Directory, below, there was not a huge selection of traditional patterns to choose from. These patterns, with a limited amount of colors, were repeated with slight variations. But there was not an extensive array of different patterning. Actually, from the large assortment of tape looms, there seems to have been more design variation in the loom itself, rather than in the tape that was woven.

The professional weavers of linen and woolen cloth kept weaving books with detailed information about their patterns. Tape weaving, on the other hand, was considered women's work, a utilitarian task, and may not have been valued enough to document and write down. Tape drafts were transmitted from one generation to the next through oral tradition and demonstration. There are no known archival examples of tape drafts in historical collections. Therefore, patterns drawn from surviving examples of historic tape are invaluable to contemporary weavers and reenactors.

These days, when rummaging at a flea market or antique shop, there is no longer much chance of finding any historical handwoven tape for sale. If you were lucky enough to find a small amount of tape, it would be extremely pricey. According to Alan Keyser, a renowned early American textile historian and author, "Today, tape from the eighteenth or nineteenth centuries could bring $50/yard, if not more."[2] It is such a paradox that this simple, everyday textile of long ago, with not much value, can bring high prices in today's market.

Warp-Faced Weaving

Handwoven tape is, for the most part, a warp-faced weave structure, with many warp threads lined up snugly next to each other. With the large number of warp threads, when a tape is cut apart, it will not fray or unweave back on itself. This feature is important since the tape would generally be woven into long lengths, stored, and cut apart for many different purposes. The strength of this weave structure also lent itself to the variety of its uses.

Traditionally, *commercially woven balanced plain weave tape* could have been used more as a

---

Grossmutter's Special Tape Pattern   *Tape Tale #4*

Passing the hemp field in my bare feet, I walked through the kitchen garden to Grossmutter's (Grandmother's) log house. While drinking some meadow tea and visiting with her, I rummaged in her rye straw yarn and tape basket. At the bottom of her basket, I was delighted to discover a bundle of linen tape in an unusual blue and brown striped pattern that I had not seen before. It was so unique that I decided I would weave this pattern and every time I used it to tie up my linen petticoat around my waist, I would remember my quiet visit with my Grossmutter.

(**Note:** The mention of the linen petticoat means this tale would have most likely taken place before the 1820s.)

Example of warp-faced handwoven linen tape, bleached and indigo dyed. Part of the Historical Tape Pattern Directory. *Collection of Susan Sharpless Messimer.*

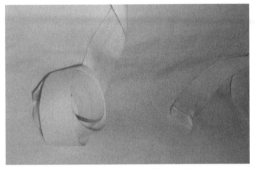

Bib apron, hand woven in bleached linen. Tape straps are commercially woven twill weave. *Collection of Landis Valley Village and Farm Museum, Pennsylvania Historical and Museum Commission.*

Top: Example of traditional contrasting, two-colored tape in typical indigo blue and bleached linen. **Bottom:** Indigo blue and brown linen. Pattern is blurred, due to similarity of dark colors, without much contrast. Notice uneven selvages. *Collection of author.*

"fancy" tape or "trim," rather than as a strong, functional tape used around the early American farms. In many cases, it would not hold up as well for heavier uses as the stronger *warp-faced woven tape* would have. (See the Historical Tape Pattern Directory in this chapter for other photos of commercially woven balanced plain weave tape.) *Commercially woven twill tape* would be a stronger fabric than the balanced plain weave tape.

In a warp-faced weave, the pattern is created solely by the color placement of the warp threads. Therefore, the different colors of the warp threads are all-important. A solid colored linen tape, all blue for example, would be functional, but there would be no color pattern involved. At least two different colors are needed to create a pattern. Contrasting colors create the most distinctive patterns. According to Ellen Gehret, "Most tapes appearing on clothing are of either a single color or two colors; occasionally a three-color tape is seen."[3] Traditional tape patterns were mostly symmetrical, with an identical pattern on the front and back. One would not usually see a rainbow of colors, nor a blending of color.

Two bundles of commercially woven cotton tape. Part of the Historical Tape Pattern Directory. *Collection of Susan Sharpless Messimer.*

No Planned Tape Usage

In general, neither tape warp colors nor patterns were planned out in advance for a specific item of clothing or any other use. That is different from today, where every color or pattern detail might be decided in advance of the making of a particular project. Ellen Gehret observes, "It is obvious from examining unused tapes in museum and private collections that many yards of tape were woven in advance of its immediate usage and that often, several weights, colors and designs were kept together on hand at the same time. There is not necessarily a relationship between the color of the garment and the color of the tape attached to it."[4] As mentioned previously, whatever they had, they used.

The Tape Pattern Draft

The tape pattern draft allows a particular pattern to be documented and then repeated when desired. As stated earlier, despite all the research done over the years, there are no known documented early American tape pattern drafts recorded, either regionally nor in individual family wills or other historical papers. Eighteenth or nineteenth century tape weavers did not write down pattern drafts for their different tape patterns.

The tape draft is an invaluable tool, giving important information to a weaver. It acts as the written map or guide to the threading order of the warp threads that are fed into the loom. By examining a section of handwoven tape, the pattern information can be transferred into a pattern draft, for easy reference and future use.

The tape pattern draft tells the total number of warp threads needed for the pattern, how many of each colored warp thread will be used, and also where to place the different colored warp threads—into which slot or hole in the rigid heddle.

The Historical Tape Pattern Directory in this chapter includes a number of tapes and their corresponding drafts. These drafts were formulated from the analysis of the actual historical tapes. Weavers that read this book will have the opportunity to replicate these tapes and continue to enjoy and pass on the tapes of the unknown tape weavers of this era, allowing these tape ties

to continue to bind, into the future.

Here is a sample tape pattern draft, describing all the important information necessary for reading a draft. Read the Warp Color Draft from left to right, from the top square to the bottom square, continuing in this sequence, top to bottom, across the entire draft, to the right side. The arrow shows the direction to read across. The black dot indicates the middle of the warp threads.

Sample Tape Pattern Draft
Tape Pattern: Simple Rib Tape Pattern
Total Warp Threads: 10
Warp Color Code & Amounts:
B – Blue (5)
W – White (5)
Warp Color Draft:

→

HOLE	B		B		B		B		B	
SLOT		W		W		W		W		W

•

(See Chapter 5 for more information on making a tape pattern draft.)

Introduction to the Historical Tape Pattern Directory

Examples of historic woven tape survive in museum collections and in the hands of individual collectors. A friend, Susan Sharpless Messimer, who found her first examples of early tape over forty years ago at a local auction, has allowed me to conduct research in her collection. We have spent many happy hours examining traditional patterns and variations in warp count and color. She has assembled a collection of over twenty examples of woven tape. To the best of my ability, I have documented these cultural artifacts from the past, including a number of the tape pattern drafts.

These small exemplars of the creativity of women are themselves part of the warp and weft of domestic history.

Although these examples' histories of ownership and use are unknown, they were all found in southeastern Pennsylvania. Many examples were found in circumstances that suggest a connection to Pennsylvania German households. They are one element of the broader study, and serve as a foundation for the Historical Tape Pattern Directory.

Handwoven Reproduction Tape from Eleanor Bittle, "The Tape Lady"

Eleanor Bittle, in eighteenth-century period clothing, as she demonstrates tape weaving at Goschenhoppen Festival, August 2009.

Many years ago, when Susan Sharpless Messimer first met Eleanor Bittle, Susan gave samples of her historical tape collection to Mrs. Bittle, who wove reproductions of the original patterns. This past year, when Susan began showing me her tape collection for my book, I realized that in addition to her historical tapes, there were a number of Eleanor Bittle's reproduced tapes present, as well.

I have included them in this tape pattern collection to compare them to the originals and also to exemplify how important the drafts can be. By following the Historic Tape Pattern Directory drafts, the reader is able to also replicate the original tapes from long ago. I am honored to be sharing some of these reproduced historical tapes, handwoven by Eleanor Bittle. They will each be identified as from Eleanor Bittle's collection of reproduced tapes.

See Appendix 1 for a list of commercial yarns appropriate for tape weaving today, including the weaving of reproduction tape.

Disclaimer

The author of this book takes full responsibility for any errors in this examination of historical cloth. Exact dates were not possible to determine for each item of this collection. The exact source of each tape sample has not been determined. There is no actual proof of the fibers or dyes used in this collection of tape. Fiber content has been determined upon examination, to the best of the

About Susan Sharpless Messimer

Susan Sharpless Messimer, a resident of Lancaster County, Pennsylvania, retired from the Pennsylvania Historical and Museum Commission after a career as a curator of historic collections. During her childhood, her parents encouraged her interest in museums. Her favorite museums are still those from her childhood visits: the Mercer Museum in Doylestown, Pennsylvania; Landis Valley Village and Farm Museum, formerly Landis Valley Museum, in Lancaster County, Pennsylvania; and the University of Pennsylvania Museum of Archaeology and Anthropology in Philadelphia.

She developed expertise in American material culture, artifact collections management, research, and exhibition design and installation. She has written articles on Americana and is a skilled demonstrator of open hearth cooking.

Susan is fascinated by technology and cultural history, in particular the history, language, and material culture of the Pennsylvania Germans. Her special focus is American textiles. Her collection of woven tape was acquired in southeastern Pennsylvania over a period of forty years. It began with a purchase of two early nineteenth century wooden holders of woven linen tape at a Conestoga Auction Company auction of a farm household in York County, Pennsylvania, in the mid-1970s. (See page 97 to view one of these two artifacts.) By frequenting local auctions and flea markets, Susan was able to buy a bundle of tape or two at a time. There really was not a lot of interest in these narrow pieces of cloth back then.

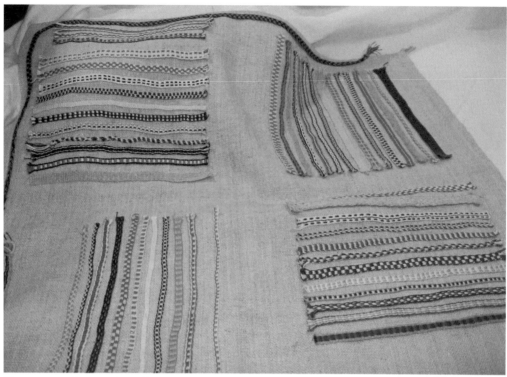

These tape samples are replicas of historic tape collected and hand woven by Eleanor Bittle. All but one are woven in linen; red rib tape in upper left quadrant is probably cotton, and is a pattern found in the Schwenkfelder Museum, Pennsburg, Pennsylvania. *Collection of Eleanor Bittle, The Tape Lady* ©.

author's ability. The collection considers the historical traditions and examination to suppose the colors.

Guide to the Historical Tape Pattern Directory

The Historical Tape Pattern Directory contains fiber information that describes a variety of handwoven tapes and their patterns, collected over a period of forty years. Tape pattern drafts have been drawn for a number of particular tapes, for study and replication.

Weave Structure
Almost all of these tape pattern samples and drafts are warp-faced weaves. Several tapes are balanced plain weave and are noted as such.

Tape Pattern Name
Hand-loomed tape was woven in a variety of widths, colors and patterns. Patterns included checkerboard, stripes, multi-stripes or solid combinations. I have given my own interpretive names to some of the patterns that are quite self-evident.

- Solid colors (no pattern)
- Checkerboard—sometimes referred to as "check." Eleanor Bittle notes, "This pattern was the most common pattern."[5]
- Stripe
- Stripe and Dash
- Dash
- Rib
- Buddha's Eye—an odd pattern, named by Susan Sharpless Messimer and author
- Balanced Plain Weave—Stripe Variations, a & b
- Fringe—Band of Fringe and Rib Variation
- Tubular weave

Individual Picture
Close-up of the tape for better examination. There may be additional information.

Bundle Picture

Quantity of handwoven tape of a particular pattern. The bundle picture notes if the tape was wrapped around a wooden tape holder, for storage.

Tape Width

Traditionally, ⅝" was usually the widest woven tape, for practical applications. Some of the tapes are very narrow, with ³⁄₁₆" to ¼" being common.

Total Warp Threads

The majority of these collected tapes are of a warp-faced weave structure. The total warp count in each tape can vary, depending on the pattern, warp thread size, and the width of the tape.

Warp Fibers

The warp fibers are predominantly handspun linen. There may be some hemp fibers, but being so similar to the linen, it would be hard to distinguish between the two fibers. There is also cotton, wool, and possibly silk.

Warp Ply

The warp threads were spun as a single-ply, 2-ply, 3-ply or 4-ply. 2-ply warp threads are the most common here.

Warp Color Code and Amounts

Explains the draft information, such as warp thread colors, their individual color code, and total amounts of each color in the pattern.

Warp Color Draft

Read from top left and down, continuing across to the right side of the page. The "holes" and "slots" contain the warp color code, depicting warp thread placement in the rigid heddle of the loom.

Weft Fiber

The weft fiber could be the same fiber as the warp or a different fiber.

Weft Ply

The weft fiber was spun as a single-ply, 2-ply, 3-ply, or 4-ply yarn.

Weft Color

Typically, the weft would be the same color as the outside or selvage warp threads. Occasionally,

Warp and Weft Thread Colors

Color analysis was not conducted for this study. Identification has been kept to basic colors, with an explanation below. See Chapter 3 for more detailed information about traditional dyes.

Natural: Linen, hemp, cotton, wool
White: Bleached linen, hemp, cotton
Blue: Indigo
Red: Madder root, Turkey red
Brown: Black walnut, other local plants

"Some tapes were of solid color. Various shades of indigo blue frequently were combined with natural or bleached linen or with brown tones. Occasionally a few strands of red were introduced into the warp."

—Ellen J. Gehret, *Rural Pennsylvania Clothing*, 1976

The smooth and slick flax fibers gave the handspun linen a limited amount of dye choices. Besides natural and bleached linen, blue or brown were the two colors that linen could absorb and that would last. Red dye did not adhere well to the flax fibers. Since cotton absorbs color much more easily than linen does, it lent itself to more color choices, such as red, once the fiber became more available in the beginning of the nineteenth century.

Variations in thread color strength may have been affected by the mordant to set the dye, weakness from the end of a dye bath, amount of time in the dye pot, or fading in light or over time.

the weft could be a contrasting color to the selvage warp threads, creating an interesting accent to the tape pattern.

Comments

All of the tapes in this collection were acquired in southeastern Pennsylvania. There is no information about the origins of the tapes and the weavers of the tapes are unknown. Any other known information is noted in this section.

HISTORICAL TAPE PATTERN DIRECTORY

1: Tape Pattern: Solid Color, Natural

Tape Width: ³⁄₁₆"   **Warp Fibers:** Linen or hemp   **Weft Fiber:** Linen or hemp
Total Warps: 11 - 13 ends   **Warp Ply:** 2-ply   **Weft ply:** 2-ply
                               Warp Color: Natural   **Weft Color:** Natural

Comments: A solid one-"colored" tape is the quickest tape to weave. Acquired in southeastern Pennsylvania.

2: Tape Pattern: Solid Color, White

Tape Width: ⅛"   **Warp Fibers:** Linen   **Weft Fiber:** Linen
Total Warps: 12   **Warp Ply:** 2-ply   **Weft ply:** 2-ply
                           Warp Color: White   **Weft Color:** White

Comments: Handwoven tape hand sewn to indigo blue and white plaid linen chaff bag. Acquired in southeastern Pennsylvania.

3: Tape Pattern: Solid Color, Blue

Tape Width: ¼"   **Warp Fibers:** Linen   **Weft Fiber:** Linen
Total Warps: 17   Warp Ply: 2-ply   Weft ply: 2-ply
                   Warp Color: Blue   Weft Color: Blue

Comments: Handwoven tape wrapped around wooden tape holder, second from top. Acquired in southeastern Pennsylvania.

4: Tape Pattern: Checkerboard

Tape Width: ³⁄₁₆"   **Warp Fibers:** Linen   **Weft Fiber:** Linen
Total Warps: 12   Warp Ply: 3-ply   Weft ply: 3-ply
                    Warp Colors: Brown, blue   Weft Color: Brown

Comments: This is a typical checkerboard pattern. "Check" was used interchangeably with "checkerboard." Checkerboard was a popular tape pattern during the eighteenth and nineteenth centuries, usually seen in blue and white and sometimes with brown tones. Acquired in southeastern Pennsylvania.

5: Tape Pattern: Checkerboard

Tape Width: ³⁄₁₆"
Total Warps: 16

Warp Fibers: Linen
Warp Ply: 2-ply
Warp Color Code & Amounts:
W – White – 8
B – Blue – 8

Weft Fiber: Linen
Weft ply: 2-ply
Weft Color: White

Warp Color Draft ⟶

HOLE	W		W		W		W		B		B		B		B
SLOT		B		B		B		B		W		W		W		W

Comments: A typical checkerboard pattern. Acquired in southeastern Pennsylvania.

6: Tape Pattern: Checkerboard Variation

Tape Width: ⅛"
Total Warps: 15

Warp Fibers: Linen, cotton
Warp Ply: 2-ply
Warp Color Code & Amounts:
B – Deep blue – 9 – linen
W – White – 2 – cotton
R – Red – 4 – cotton

Weft Fiber: Linen
Weft ply: 3-ply
Weft Color: Blue

Warp Color Draft ⟶

HOLE	B		R		R		W		W		R		R		B
SLOT		B		B		B		B		B		B		B	

Comments: Both warp and weft threads were very thinly spun. This variation of checkerboard has three sections of checkerboard, not two. Acquired in southeastern Pennsylvania.

7: **Tape Pattern:** Checkerboard Variation

Tape Width: ⅛"   **Warp Fibers:** Linen   **Weft Fiber:** Linen
Total Warps: 6   Warp Ply: Unknown, hemmed ends   Weft ply: Unknown
                        Warp Color: Blue, white   Weft Color: White

Comments: This pattern is a very subtle checkerboard, hand sewn to linen plaid bolster. Acquired in southeastern Pennsylvania.

8: **Tape Pattern:** Solid Stripe

Tape Width: ⅛"   **Warp Fibers:** Linen   **Weft Fiber:** Linen
Total Warps: 9   Warp Ply: Unknown, hemmed ends   Weft ply: Unknown, hemmed ends
                        Warp Color Code & Amounts: Weft Color: White
                        W – White – 6
                        B – Blue – 3

Warp Color Draft ⟶

HOLE	W		W		B		W		W
SLOT		W		B		B		W	

Comments: Handwoven tape hand sewn to linen check chaff bag. Acquired in southeastern Pennsylvania.

9: Tape Pattern: Three Solid Stripes / Band of Fringe

Tape Width: ³⁄₁₆"
Total Warps: 16

Warp Fibers: Linen, cotton, possible silk
Warp Ply: 2-ply
Warp Color Code & Amounts:
G – Gold – 4 – possible silk
B – Blue – 8 – linen
W – White – 4 – cotton

Weft Fiber: Wool
Weft ply: 2-ply
Weft Color: Fringe: Red, purple, gold, pale green

Warp Color Draft ⟶

HOLE	G		B		B		W		W		B		B		G	
SLOT		G		B		B		W		W		B		B		G

Comments: Tape side fringe, with warp-faced tape header. Gold selvage warp threads, thin shimmering thread, possibly silk. Different wool weft colors peeking through one selvage. Other selvage has four sets of colored wool as fringe, which has faded. Acquired in southeastern Pennsylvania, possibly in York County. See page 106, "Band of Fringe," for bundle of fringe, and page 187 for instructions on weaving tape side fringe.

10: Tape Pattern: Three Solid Stripes

Tape Width: ³⁄₈"
Total Warps: 9

Warp Fibers: Linen
Warp Ply: Unknown, hemmed ends
Warp Colors: Light blue, deep brown, natural

Weft Fiber: Linen
Weft ply: Unknown, hemmed ends
Weft Color: Light blue

Comments: Tape ties hand sewn to indigo blue and bleached linen check apron waistband, possibly ironed, since very flat. Acquired in southeastern Pennsylvania, probably Lancaster County.

11: Tape Pattern: Multiple Stripes

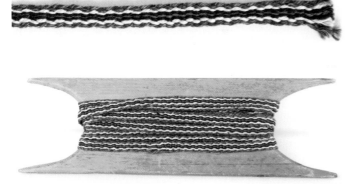

Tape Width: ¼"
Total Warps: 14

Warp Fibers: Linen, cotton
Warp Ply: 2 ply
Warp Color Code & Amounts:
B – Blue – 4 – linen
W – White – 4 – cotton
DB – Dark blue – 4 – linen
BN – Brown – 2 – linen

Weft Fiber: Linen
Weft ply: 2-ply
Weft Color: Medium blue

Warp Color Draft ⟶

HOLE	B		W		DB		BN		DB		W		B	
SLOT		B		W		DB		BN		DB		W		B

Comments: Tape bundle wrapped around a wooden tape holder. See Eleanor Bittle's handwoven linen reproduction of this original tape on page 109. Acquired in southeastern Pennsylvania.

12: Tape Pattern: Stripe/Dash Combo

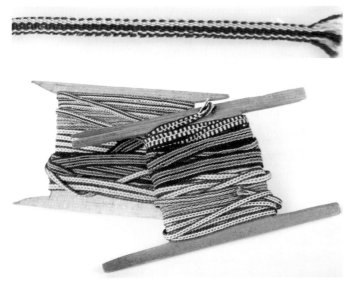

Tape Width: ³⁄₁₆"
Total Warps: 14

Warp Fibers: Linen
Warp Ply: 2-ply
Warp Color Code & Amounts:
B – Dark blue – 7
W – White – 7

Weft Fiber: Linen
Weft ply: 2-ply
Weft Color: White

Warp Color Draft ⟶

HOLE	B		W		B		B		W		W		W	
SLOT		B		W		B		B		W		W		B

Comments: This asymmetrical tape pattern was not a common pattern in the eighteenth and nineteenth centuries. The lower photo shows this original tape pattern wrapped around top of rear wooden tape holder. Eleanor Bittle's handwoven linen reproduction of this original tape is seen in the photo on page 109. Acquired in southeastern Pennsylvania.

13: Tape Pattern: Single Dash

Tape Width: ¼"
Total Warps: 13

Warp Fibers: Linen
Warp Ply: 2-ply
Warp Color Code & Amounts:
B – Blue – 4
W – White – 8
R – Red – 1, top and blue, middle

Weft Fiber: Linen
Weft ply: 2-ply
Weft Color: Natural

Warp Color Draft ⟶

HOLE	B		W		W		R		W		B	
SLOT		B		W		W		W		W		B

Comments: Top two reproduction tapes, hand woven by Eleanor Bittle. This was a very common pattern in the eighteenth and nineteenth centuries. See original tape in lower photo under Tape Pattern 12, two tapes on both wooden tape holders. Acquired in southeastern Pennsylvania.

14: Tape Pattern: Single Dash with Border

Tape Width: ¼"
Total Warps: 13

Warp Fibers: Cotton
Warp Ply: 2-ply
Warp Color Code & Amounts:
P – Pink – 4
B – Blue – 4
W – White – 4
R – Red – 1

Weft Fiber: Linen
Weft ply: 2-ply
Weft Color: Natural

Warp Color Draft ⟶

HOLE	P		B		W		R		W		B		P
SLOT		P		B		W		W		B		P	

Comments: This is a reproduction tape, unknown weaver. Notice the linen accent weft showing on the selvages. See Eleanor Bittle's linen reproduction of this pattern on page 109. Acquired in southeastern Pennsylvania

15: Tape Pattern: Double Dash with Border

Tape Width: ¼"   Warp Fibers: Linen   Weft Fiber: Linen
Total Warps: 13   Warp Ply: 2-ply   Weft ply: 2-ply
                        Warp Colors: Brown, white, blue   Weft Color: Brown

Comments: Reproduction tape, hand woven by Eleanor Bittle. Acquired in southeastern Pennsylvania.

16: Tape Pattern: Double Dash Variation

Tape Width: ⁵⁄₁₆"   Warp Fibers: Cotton   Weft Fiber: Linen
Total Warps: 11   Warp Ply: 4-ply   Weft ply: 3-ply
                        Warp Colors: Blue, pink, brown, red, green   Weft Color: Natural

Comments: Unusual amount of warp thread colors. Notice how the weft thread floats over green warp thread periodically, in center of tape. Acquired in southeastern Pennsylvania.

17: **Tape Pattern:** Triple Dash

Tape Width: ⁵⁄₁₆"
Total Warps: 7

Warp Fibers: Wool
Warp Ply: 2-ply
Warp Color Code & Amounts:
G – Deep green – 4
R – Red – 2
W – White – 1

Weft Fiber: Wool
Weft ply: 2 ply
Weft Color: Green

Warp Color Draft ⟶

HOLE	G		G		G		G
SLOT		R		W		R	

Comments: All wool tape. Acquired in southeastern Pennsylvania.

18: **Tape Pattern:** Simple Rib

Tape Width: ⅛"
Total Warps: 8

Warp Fibers: Linen
Warp Ply: Unknown, hemmed ends
Warp Color Code & Amounts:
B – Blue – 4
W – White – 4

Weft Fiber: Linen
Weft ply: Unknown, hemmed ends
Weft Color: White

Warp Color Draft ⟶

HOLE	B		B		B		B	
SLOT		W		W		W		W

Comments: Handwoven tape ties hand sewn to cotton plaid waistband on calico cotton petticoat. Acquired in southeastern Pennsylvania.

19: Tape Pattern: Simple Rib

Tape Width: ⅛"
Total Warps: 11

Warp Fibers: Linen
Warp Ply: 2-ply
Warp Color: Blue and white

Weft Fiber: Linen
Weft ply: 2-ply
Weft Color: White

Comments: Handwoven tape ties hand sewn to check chaff bag. Acquired in southeastern Pennsylvania.

20: Tape Pattern: Rib with Stripe

Tape Width: ¼"
Total Warps: 16

Warp Fibers: Linen, cotton
Warp Ply: Linen 2-ply, cotton 4-ply
Warp Color Code & Amounts:
B – Blue – 8
N – Natural – 6
P – Pink – 2, cotton

Weft Fiber: Linen
Weft ply: 2-ply
Weft Color: Natural

Warp Color Draft ⟶

HOLE	B		B		B		B		P		N		N		N	
SLOT		N		N		N		P		B		B		B		B

Comments: Handwoven tape ties hand sewn to tow linen twill grain bag with knot. Acquired in southeastern Pennsylvania.

21: Tape Pattern: Band of Fringe

Tape Width: ³⁄₁₆"; Fringe: 1¼"

Weft Fiber: Wool fringe
Weft ply: 2-ply
Weft Colors: Fringe: Red, purple, gold, pale green.
Four complete weft sets per color.

Comments: Bundle of side tape fringe, probably to be attached as "trim" to accessories, wrapped around wide wooden board. Different wool weft colors peeking through top selvage. Bottom selvage has four sets (two weft shots each) of colored wool, as fringe, which has faded. Acquired in southeastern Pennsylvania, possibly in York County.

See page 100 for side fringe weaving information.

22: Tape Pattern: Coverlet Tape Fringe, Standard Rib

Tape Width: ½"; Fringe: 3½"
Total Warps: 10

Warp Fibers: Cotton, wool
Warp Ply: Unknown, hemmed ends
Warp Colors: Tan cotton, red wool

Weft Fiber: Wool
Weft ply: 2-ply
Weft Color: Fringe: Red, gold, deep blue, green

Comments: Handwoven, nineteenth century coverlet, wool and cotton. Weaver was Samuel Gilbert, Trappe, Montgomery County, Pennsylvania, 1853. Handwoven "Attached Bottom" tape fringe of wool and cotton. Balanced plain weave or 50/50 weave, hand sewn to bottom of coverlet. Twenty-four color sets as weft fringe, on one side only. Notice slight unraveling of hand stitching of tape fringe to coverlet. Acquired in southeastern Pennsylvania. See page 110 for detailed coverlet fringe information.

23: Tape Pattern: Buddha's Eye

Tape Width: ⅜"
Total Warps: 17

Warp Fibers: Wool, linen
Warp Ply: 2-ply wool, single-ply linen
Warp Colors:
Natural linen
Pale green wool
Indigo blue wool
Red wool; appears to be plied with
natural linen, creating speckled effect
Black (deep indigo?) wool

Weft Fiber: Wool
Weft ply: 2-ply
Weft Color: Pale green

Comments: Handwoven wool and linen tape bundle wrapped tightly around a wooden cigar box lid. Knot in center of bundle could have possibly been a broken warp thread, knotted with linen warp thread, and weaving continued. Name given by author and Susan Sharpless Messimer. Acquired in southeastern Pennsylvania.

24: Tape Pattern: Balanced Plain Weave, Stripe (handwoven, most likely)

Tape Width: ⅝"
Total Warps: 22

Warp Fibers: Linen, cotton
Warp Ply: 2-ply
Warp Colors: Blue and white linen, red cotton

Weft Fiber: Linen
Weft ply: 2-ply
Weft Color: Blue, deep indigo

Comments: Tape appears to be a handwoven balanced plain weave, but woven poorly, since the selvages are quite ragged. See page 101 for a photo of this tape wrapped around both wooden tape holders. See page 91 for information comparing warp-faced and balanced plain weave structures. Acquired in southeastern Pennsylvania.

25: Tape Pattern: Balanced Plain Weave, Stripe

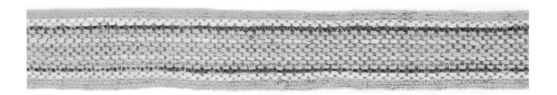

Tape Width: ¾"   **Warp Fibers:** Cotton, commercially spun   **Weft Fiber:** Cotton, commercially spun
Total Warps: 40   Warp Ply: Single-ply   Weft ply: Single-ply
                   Warp Colors: Tan, natural, dark brown   Weft Color: Tan

Comments: Tape was commercially woven, probably as "trim" tape. Balanced plain weave. See page 91 for a photo of two bundles of this tape. Acquired in southeastern Pennsylvania.

26: Tape Pattern: Tubular Cordage

Tape Width: ⅛"   **Warp Fibers:** Linen or hemp   **Weft Fiber:** Linen or hemp
Total Warps: 12   Warp Ply: 2-ply   Weft ply: 2-ply
                   Warp Color: Natural   Weft Color: Natural

Comments: Four stacked bundles of linen or hemp tubular cordage. See page 114 for historical information and page 90 for instructions on weaving tubular cordage. Acquired in southeastern Pennsylvania.

27: **Tape Pattern:** Eleanor Bittle Reproduction Tapes, for tape patterns 12, Stripe Dash Combo and 11, Multiple Stripe

Tape Width: ¼"
Total Warps: 14

Warp Fibers: Linen
Warp Ply: 2-ply
Warp Colors: (12) white, blue;
(11) Blue, white, brown

Weft Fiber: Linen
Weft ply: 2-ply
Weft Color: Natural

Comments: Eleanor Bittle, known as "The Tape Lady" in southeastern Pennsylvania, is an educator of Pennsylvania German tape weaving.

The following three collection tapes have not been examined but are included as items of interest.

Colonial Tape Fringe for Coverlets and "Trim"

All over the world, handwoven tape fringe has been woven for hundreds of years. Europe saw an enormous amount, with Italy and Spain known for their fringe in the seventeenth century, followed by France with beautiful silk fringe. Handwoven fringe had a large array of uses, from curtains, toweling, napkins, coverlet and rug edges, and upholstery, to clothing and apron trim.[6] Commercially woven fringe could be bought in shops, especially in the large cities, like Philadelphia.

During the early American period, there was a variety of fringe that was handwoven, either for coverlets, woven on the large barn looms by the professional weavers, or on the small "trim" or "fringe" tape looms for smaller textiles.

Silk tape fringe on window hanging, c. 1780. *Courtesy of Winterthur Museum. Museum purchase.*

Quilt dated 1830, made in either Bucks or Lehigh County, Pennsylvania. No information about tape fringe. Tape header appears to be warp-faced, probably woven on barn loom. Hand stitched to quilt. Notice the elaborate fringe and tassels. *Collection of Winterthur Museum.*

Early American Coverlet Fringe

American bed coverlets were very popular during the eighteenth and nineteenth centuries. Most settlers would have a skilled weaver make their coverlets, in geometric patterns. In the later transition to the Jacquard looms of the nineteenth century, coverlets were woven in the more complex curvilinear patterned textiles.

Many coverlets from this time period would have a fringe, including tape, bound to three sides. The top edge was usually rolled into a hem. This was practical, since the top portion of the coverlet would be pulled close to the user's face. Getting a mouthful of fringe while sleeping would be quite "distasteful."

Side or Weft Fringe

During the weaving process on the barn loom, the wool weft would be woven beyond the actual coverlet, wrapping around strong supplemental warps on each side and looped back into the fabric. This created blocks of colored wool as side fringe, the same colors as the woven coverlet sections.[7]

Warp Fringe

These coverlets were woven with many long warp ends that made a thick finished fringe at the bottom, also woven on the barn loom. Warp fringe for the bottom of the coverlet was the usual finishing technique in complex point work coverlets.[8]

Attached Tape Fringe, Separately Woven

This type of coverlet fringe became an important edging technique that was hand-sewn to a variety of coverlets during the colonial period. It would normally be woven on a barn loom by a professional weaver and made a fancy and interesting finish to a coverlet. The traditional tape fringe consisted of wool or wool and cotton threads woven in as the weft, in a manner that created a fringe on one edge only. The Pennsylvania Germans produced this type of separately woven, attached fringe and used it on their woven coverlets.[9]

Nineteenth century geometric coverlet in Summer and Winter pattern. Coverlet tape fringe surrounds the sides and bottom of coverlet. An example of "attached sides and bottom tape fringe," in twill pattern. Tape fringe sewn onto coverlet with small overcast stitches, using fine wool or cotton. Coverlet bought at antique shop in Bedford, Pennsylvania. *Collection of Gay McGeary.*

Warp-Faced Weave Header and Balanced Plain Weave Header

In the *Attached* tape fringe, the tape acts as the header or basic cloth base for the fringe to hang off from. There are two types of tape headers, warp-faced and 50/50 or balanced plain weave. With their different characteristics, they would be attached to a coverlet for finishing the edges, depending on which type preferred. Both make equally attractive fringe edges.

Warp-Faced Weave Header consists of the tape warp threads being pulled snugly next to each other. Only the warp threads would be seen. This technique is much stronger than the 50/50 or balanced plain weave header. See below for examples.

Balanced Plain Weave Header has an equal amount of warps as weft and was sometimes referred to as 50/50 coverlet tape fringe. One can see the equal distanced warp and weft threads, from row to row. When weaving this type of tape header, the weaver would not pull in the weft as

tightly. It was not as strong as the warp-faced header, but had a nice finished look.

Attached Sides and Bottom tape fringe needed a long length of tape to be woven and sewn on three sides of a coverlet.

Warp-faced Weave Header Samples

Nineteenth century geometric coverlet pattern called Star and Diamond. Coverlet tape fringe surrounds sides and bottom of coverlet. An example of "attached sides and bottom tape fringe," in warp-faced weave. Tape fringe sewn onto coverlet with small overcast stitches, using fine wool or cotton. Coverlet was bought on eBay in 2011. Dealer is L. Becker, Vintage Linen, Lace and Textiles from Kulpsville, Pennsylvania. *Collection of Gay McGeary.*

Close-up of Star and Diamond coverlet. Shows detail of "attached" tape fringe, hand sewn around the corner of coverlet, as well as warp-faced structure. *Collection of Gay McGeary.*

Tape fringe, Overshot Ivy. Nineteenth century geometric coverlet pattern is Overshot Tree pattern. Coverlet tape fringe surrounds sides and bottom of coverlet. Another example of "attached sides and bottom tape fringe," in warp-faced weave. Tape fringe sewn onto coverlet with small overcast stitches, using fine wool or cotton. Coverlet purchased from Ivy Hall, Abbottstown, Pennsylvania, 2012. *Collection of Gay McGeary.*

Balanced Plain Weave Header Samples
Attached Bottom tape fringe was another choice, with a much shorter amount of tape fringe that was hand sewn to just the bottom of the coverlet. (See page 106 for more information about this coverlet example.)

Nineteenth century geometric coverlet pattern called Nine Star. Tape fringe surrounds sides and bottom of coverlet. An example of "attached sides and bottom tape fringe," in balanced plain weave or 50/50 weave tape pattern. Sewn onto coverlet with small overcast stitches, using fine wool or cotton. Coverlet purchased from School House Farm Antiques, New Holland, Pennsylvania, 2008. *Collection of Gay McGeary.*

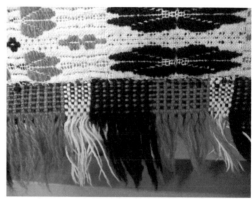

Nineteenth century geometric coverlet has tape fringe in balanced plain weave or 50/50 weave tape pattern. Sewn onto coverlet with small overcast stitches, using fine wool or cotton. *Private collection.*

Nineteenth century coverlet, jacquard woven with "bottom tape fringe." Fringe is warp-faced weave, sewn onto coverlet with small overcast stitches, using fine wool or cotton. See page 106 in Historical Tape Pattern Directory for more information about coverlet. *Collection of Susan Sharpless Messimer.*

Binder Weft

The binder weft is a very thin weft thread, such as sewing thread, that is woven in the same shed as the fringe weft. It should be the same color as the selvage warps so that it is not noticed. The binder weft stops the warp threads from unraveling at the bottom edge, sliding into the fringe area.

There seems to be a discussion as to whether or not a binder weft thread was woven into the tape fringe attached to the edges of traditional coverlets. One authority states that it was used, but in examining old coverlets, I have not seen any. This seems to be a more modern practice. Gay McGeary added that that she "does not think it was used historically." When I asked why not, Gay replied, "If a coverlet was hand washed after

Close-up of Nine Star coverlet, somewhat unraveling at edge of tape fringe. A binder thread was not woven into fringe when made, which could cause this to happen. *Collection of Gay McGeary.*

Close-up of tape fringe, Overshot Ivy, somewhat unraveling at edge of tape fringe. A binder thread not woven into fringe when made, which could cause this to happen. *Collection of Gay McGeary.*

woven, the piece, including the tape fringe, would felt a little, binding the ends together."[10] I wonder if it could also have been a time saver to skip the additional work of weaving in a binder thread.

The above examples of coverlet fringe are woven of wool or wool and cotton. Linen was not being used at this later time period, in the early nineteenth century, having died out with the advent of milled cotton. See Appendix 2 for a list of coverlet weaving books that discuss floor loom tape fringe weaving.

Gay McGeary, a Coverlet Weaver

Gay McGeary has been weaving, collecting, and researching early coverlet patterns and weave structures for over twenty-five years. While her weaving is inspired by her research, her research is enhanced by her weaving explorations of the early craftspeople. Gay sees each coverlet as a work of art, a living statement from the past, of color, design, and texture, inviting you into the mind of the artisan who created it.[11]

Left: Gay McGeary, displaying a number of her handwoven coverlets. She makes her own coverlet tape fringe for her individual coverlets. *Courtesy of Gay McGeary.*

Right: Sample of Gay McGeary's wool tape fringe, woven in balanced plain weave pattern, on her large floor loom, for one of her handwoven coverlets. Notice fringe is made from wrapping weft thread around a few warp threads several inches to the right of woven tape header. Fringe will be trimmed at end and then header will be hand sewn to coverlet edges. *Courtesy of Gay McGeary.*

Weaving (Tape Side) Fringe on a "Fringe" or "Trim" Tape Loom

Side fringe was woven on the popular "fringe" or "trim" tape looms. This type of tape fringe was probably seen more often on "English" textiles, such as napkins, upholstery, curtains and drapery, aprons and pocketbooks. As with the coverlet fringe, the warp-faced tape fringe would be stronger than the 50/50 quality tape fringe. It really depended upon the purpose and use for the finished fringe. (See page 16 in Chapter 1 to view the picture of Governor Mifflin's wife, Sarah, at her "fringe" loom.)

See page 33 for pictures of tape side fringe on pocketbook from Winterthur museum. See Chapter 7 for instructions in weaving tape side fringe on a tape loom.

Replicated samples of tubular tow and linen cordage, woven by Eleanor Bittle. Eleanor mentioned to me that she spent some time making large number of woven corded curtain ties for windows at Peter Wentz House; a lot of cordage!

Example of handwoven warp-faced tape fringe. Tape fringe woven on a box or standing, floor tape loom. Different colors of dyed wool woven for weft fringe. See page 106 in Historical Tape Pattern Directory for more information about this tape fringe. *Collection of Susan Sharpless Messimer.*

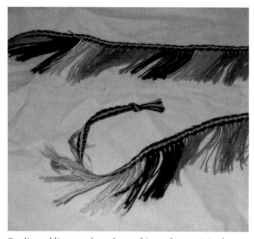

Replicated linen and wool tape fringe, from original fringe sample. Hand woven by Eleanor Bittle, on standing tape loom. She feels the standing tape loom gives the weaver more control over fringe making.

Historical Tubular Cordage

Being strong and functional, there were numerous uses for tubular cordage during the early American period. Examples would be drawstrings for satchels and bags, as well as for curtain drapery.

Woven cordage is made with one shuttle repeatedly being woven in only one direction. See page 190 in Chapter 7 for complete instructions. It is an interesting technique and weaves up quickly.

Finishing and Storing of Early American Handwoven Tape

"There were no set rules. Whatever a family member decided to do with that particular tape, knotted or hemmed, is what they did."[12] These comments by Mrs. Bittle are a good reminder that the different finishing and storing methods for tape really depended on the purpose, as well as how the tape weaver wanted to finish it. These are simply choices that the families had after the tape was cut from the loom and collected for future uses.

The Finishing of the Tape Ends

- *Hemmed tape ends.* This was a very common way of securing the tape ends. It took a little time, but was a tidy finish, with no warp threads showing. All of the warp ends were simply tucked under, rolled into a tight hem and sewn in place, using a linen or cotton thread.

- *Overhand-knotted tape ends.* I asked Eleanor Bittle about finishing the tape. She responded, "Probably more tape (was finished) with overhand knots. They would be quicker."[13] This technique was much quicker than hemming, but did not give as refined a finish as a hemmed tape end.

- *Braided tape ends.* This finishing method demonstrates how resourceful traditional tape weavers were, by using as much of the warp threads as possible. At the end of a weaving project, there was a length of warp threads left over from initially tying them on to the back of the loom. Instead of discarding these warp threads, a weaver could cut the end of the project close to the original knot and use these threads as part of the tape, by twisting them into a braid. This braiding would extend the length of the total tape. Eleanor Bittle told me that she "has seen more of this, for added length, and [they] usually would have been six-inch lengths."[14]

Section of traditional tape that had been tied to an old potato grader. Hand woven in natural gray, indigo dyed linen, and natural cotton. Tape end braided, for added length. *Private collection.*

Storing the Woven Tape

Handwoven tape could easily get lost or wear out from use, so it would continuously be woven and stored for future purposes. "Many yards [of tape] were kept on hand, usually stored in traditional rye straw baskets, with the rye grown on the farm and made into a basket. Perhaps if the farmer or

From Susan Sharpless Messimer's tape collection, bundle of natural linen cordage. See page 108 in Historical Tape Pattern Directory for details. *Collection of Susan Sharpless Messimer.*

his wife needed a garter or required a tape for a seed bag or apron string, a piece, the correct length, was cut from the most appropriate hank available in the basket."[15] They could store their bundles of tape in the basket, as well as shorter lengths and some linen thread, ready for another tape project.

Wrapping the Family Tape for Storage

Considering that much of the tape was made up of many yards, these wrapping methods were very practical in keeping the bundles of tape orderly and secure for storing:

- The tape length could be wrapped in many layers around itself, in approximately a 5-inch long bundle. The bundle could then be held in place by tying the end of the tape around the bundle several times, securing it tightly.
- The tape could be folded into a 5- to 6-inch size and wrapped around the fold a number of times. A straight pin could hold the bundle in place.
- Tape could easily be wrapped into a ball, similar to wrapping a ball of rags, and secured with a straight pin or tucked into the ball.

Eleanor Bittle's reproduced tape, woven mostly in linen, showing different manners of storing it. A simple straight pin keeps tape all together.

Several different styles of wooden holders were used to wrap a quantity of tape for storage. Usually they were hand carved, with concave indentations on each end to make the wrapping of tape an easy task. A straight pin could hold the bundle in place or the tape end could simply be tucked into the bundle.

I've heard of two other names for these holders. "Wooden stretcher" is a name used by Clarke Hess in his book *Mennonite Arts*.[16] Eleanor Bittle

Handmade rye straw basket filled with bundles of handwoven tape, along with wooden tape holder. Also strickt of linen and bundle of linen thread. *Basket belongs to author. Tape and linen, Collection of Susan Sharpless Messimer.*

Handmade rye straw basket filled with wooden tape holders or winders. Basket belongs to author. Tape in Historical Tape Pattern Directory. *Collection of Susan Sharpless Messimer.*

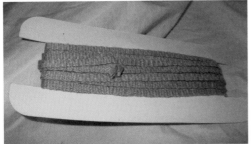

Reproduced linen tape, hand woven by Eleanor Bittle, with her reproduction cardboard tape "winder" to collect tape.

Cutting Off and Using the Stored Tape

When a family member needed a piece of tape for a lost stocking garter or boy's hat band, the mother could have gone to the rye straw basket and cut off the amount needed from a bundle, wooden holder, or ball of tape. Being a warp-faced weave structure, it would not fray (other than the weft thread, at the end) or unweave, as a balanced plain weave would have. That is part of the beauty of these long, thin bands of cloth. The family tape was very strong, stored easily in bundles, balls or holders, and was simply cut off as needed for many different purposes. No wonder miles and miles of tape were woven by many settler families during the eighteenth and early nineteenth centuries.

calls them "winders," winding the tape around the "winder."[17] She makes her own "winders" out of strong cardboard, to store much of her reproduction tape. A good woodworker could replicate that into a wooden holder that would be traditional, as well as quite useful.

PART TWO

Contemporary Tape Weaving

5. Warping the Tape Loom

Samples of contemporary thread that work well for tape weaving. Far left: black cottolin, above, light green linen, bottom green, Tencel, orange cotton carpet warp, tan hemp, and deep green, 3/2 perle cotton. (5/2 perle cotton, not shown, also works well.) All are strong and smooth, which is important in handwoven tape thread.

The Warp Threads

A warp-faced weaving emphasizes the warp threads, with all of them pulled snug, close together, from row to row. They are the only threads seen in the finished tape. The weft thread is completely hidden inside of the warp threads, but does peak out at the edges, or selvages.

The warp threads need to be smooth and quite strong. They are the threads doing most of the work, moving up and down in the rigid heddle. There are some beautiful fibers that can be used for tape weaving. Linen, hemp, cotton, cottolin, and Tencel are good choices. For a beginning weaver, though, I recommend strong cotton for

the warp threads, such as cotton carpet warp. Black warp threads tend to be weaker, from the dyeing process; something to think about if putting on a very long set of warp threads. If the warps are weak, put them through the holes, not slots, if the pattern allows. Or use the weaker threads for the weft, where they won't be strained. See Appendix 1 for yarn standards.

Warp Thread Colors Define the Pattern

A solid, one "color" tape is the easiest to warp on a loom. After determining the length and amount of warp threads, simply measure the lengths of the solid color and feed them through the loom. There is technically no pattern, so no draft is necessary.

As described in Chapter 4, to create a pattern for a tape weaving, at least two sets of different colored warp threads are needed. The pattern is determined by the color sequence of the warps. The pattern is much more distinct if the warp thread colors are contrasting.

Calculating the Warp Threads

It can be fun to create your own tape pattern and translate it into the pattern draft. If specific dimensions are desired for a tape, there is a simple formula that can help. Once the final length has been decided, there are two questions that need to be answered:

The Out-of-Order Warp Threads
Tape Tale #5

How I love our warm, sunny summer days, especially when I don't have to be inside cleaning, cleaning, cleaning. The weather was so nice outside that I decided to warp our family tape loom on the bench, under the tree, just outside of our log house. Oh my, those geese really need to be penned in! When I ran back into the house to get my scissors, those pesky geese ruined my warp threads on the loom, by pecking and pulling on them. The threads landed all over the ground, dirty and out of order. After measuring out another set of warp threads, I decided it would be quicker to simply cut off the dirty threads hanging in front of the rigid heddle and tie the new warp threads directly to them. Then I'd pull them all throught the heddle and wind the new ones to the back of the loom. Quicker than starting all over. And, I penned up the geese before I returned to working on the loom!

- What is the *working* length of each warp thread?
- What is the total amount of warp ends?

Finding the Length of Each Warp Thread

As with any handweaving project, the final length of the weaving does not tell the initial length of the warp threads. To calculate the accurate length, there are several factors that need to be taken into consideration—take up and shrinkage, finishing (any fringe or hem), and loom waste.

- Take up and Shrinkage: Take up is the added length needed for warp threads to go over and under the weft threads. Shrinkage occurs during off-loom washing (I usually don't wash my tape.) Usually this combined number is 20% of the total length.
- Finishing (fringe or hem): If weaving only one tape, it is accounted for in the loom waste. If weaving several tapes, fringe or hem amounts are measured between the tapes.
- Loom waste: 15". Waste comes from the warp threads tied to the front and back of the loom that cannot be woven.

Here's an example of how to find the length of each warp end for a tape that's to be 100" long.

Finished length: ....100"
Take up and Shrinkage *(20%)*: ....20"
Fringe or Hems *(both ends)*: ....0"
Loom Waste: ....15"
+ _____
Length of Each Warp End: ....135"

Finding the Total Number of Warp Ends

The total number of warp threads depends on the width of the finished tape *or* the tape pattern and draft. If you are following a draft, the total warp ends are given. But if you are creating an original draft, with a specific desired width, this can be tricky. Because the tape is warp-faced, there could be up to twice as many warp threads as in a balanced weave. But only half are showing on each side. It can be confusing, indeed.

Warp See(e)d Studio

My studio sign has traveled with me, over the years, to many indoor and outdoor art and craft shows. I wove the lettering in hemp and cotton, on one of my box tape looms. The spelling of the word "seeed" is intentional. When coming into my weaving booth and glancing at my studio name, I would often hear comments of "Warp Speed Studio." After informing visitors of the correct name too many times, I decided to change it to "Seeed," to emphasize the real name, tongue-in-cheek. Then everyone got it!

The name of my hand weaving studio, Warp Seed Studio, came about from my initial understanding of warp threads. As a new weaver I learned, the hard way (of course), the importance of warp placement and consistent warp tension. Otherwise, problems can arise. If even one warp thread gets out of line, or becomes too loose or tight, it needs to be adjusted before proceeding. To me, the warp threads are the core, or seed, of any weaving project. I am quite protective of them and want all the warps to be happy!

Calculate the number of warp threads wrapped around a ruler, for an inch. (Wrap snugly.) Double that number and multiply by the finished width desired. Of course, there are a number of variables in the threads themselves, such as twist, thickness, and softness of fiber. I highly recommend sampling and experimenting. Experience will teach what amount of warp ends work best for certain widths.

Remember, the width also depends on the rigid heddle. How many slots and holes determine the maximum tape width allowed, usually no more than forty.

Odd Number of Warp Threads

The number of warp threads depends on the width of the finished tape or the tape pattern and draft. It is more practical to have an odd number of warp threads as the total. By doing so, the middle slot or hole in the heddle will hold the "odd" thread.

When working with a pattern that has an even number of warp threads, such as 24, there are two solutions.

- The pattern could be adapted to allow for 23 or 25 threads.
- Or, keep the even number of threads. When threading the heddle, there will be one more thread on one side, than on the other. That is okay and will not make a difference in the final woven tape. Do not have *all* the warp threads on one side of the heddle, though, but balanced from the middle of the heddle and out on each side.

The Tape Pattern

In order to plot the sequence of colored warp threads onto the warp color draft, for the pattern, all of the warp thread information must be gathered. After choosing the threads, the tape pattern, and now knowing the amount of warp threads needed, a warp color draft can be made with the information that has been obtained.

> ## Warp Thread Information Needed to Create a Warp Color Draft
>
> - The total number of warp threads.
> - The total number of each warp thread color.
> - The warp pattern color code, which is the sequence of colored warp thread placement in the rigid heddle.

Prepare the Warp Color Draft Grid

Here are three choices of draft grids to hold the draft information.

- Graph paper: Mark two sets of horizontal lines across the graph paper with a ruler, for the length needed.
- Draw the draft grid: Using a ruler, draw the grid, with two sets of long horizontal lines and short vertical lines separating the different cells.
- Create a computer table template.

See Appendix 4 for templates.

Sample Tape Pattern and Warp Color Draft

Tape Pattern: Simple Rib
  Total Warp Threads: 10
  Warp Color Code & Amounts:
                              B – Blue (5)
                              W – White (5)

Warp Color Draft

HOLE	B		B		B		B		B	
SLOT		W		W		W		W		W

Read from *left to right,* from the top cell to the bottom cell, continuing in this sequence, across the entire draft. The arrow shows the direction to read across. The black dot shows the middle of the pattern, which can help when counting warp threads.

This same draft may also be written in a tighter format. That's especially useful if there are many warp threads and space on a page is an issue. The pattern draft below is stating the same information as the above draft.

→

HOLE	B	B	B	B	B
SLOT	W	W	W	W	W

•

Prepare the Tape Pattern Chart

In addition to the warp color *draft,* to really visualize the finished tape pattern, a tape pattern *chart* allows the pattern to come alive. It is a simple warp-color "draw down." By charting six rows of weaving, alternating between the "slot" and "hole" rows, the contrasting colors are really defined. A pattern chart may be created first, and then the colors plugged into the warp color draft; whichever works better.

Here is the tape pattern chart for the above sample pattern draft. The arrow means to read up.

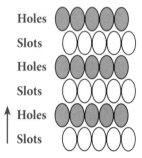

Holes
Slots
Holes
Slots
↑ Holes
Slots

Measuring the Warp Threads

Measuring a warp for a tape loom is similar to measuring a warp for a large floor loom, but on a smaller scale. Hang your warping board at a comfortable level and begin measuring your warp threads. There are a few supplies needed:

- The tape pattern and draft
- A tape measure
- Scissors
- Warp thread
- Scrap yarn

The Warping Board

This is a functional piece of equipment used to measure the warp threads for each weaving project. If there is no warping board handy, there are alternative ways to measure your warp threads, which I will discuss briefly at the end of this section. A warping board is a good investment. It is especially practical if you are thinking of exploring other types of weave structures, which involve many more warp threads. It is quick and easy to use. It can be hung on a wall, out of the way. And, it's a great display rack for scarves, hats, or other interesting items in between weaving projects!

Guide String

The guide string is a helpful tool, showing the path of the warp threads being wrapped around the dowels on the warping board. It is used to measure the length of each of the warps (warp threads). Chose a thread that is a contrasting color to the warps. That makes it easy to identify when pulling all the threads from the warping board.

1. Using a tape measure, measure the guide string the length of one warp thread, adding about 6" to that number, for tying around the top and bottom dowels.

2. Tie the guide string to the top left dowel, using an overhand knot.

3. Going to the right, as you enter the *cross section*, take the guide string UNDER the first dowel and OVER the second dowel. The *cross* is very important. It keeps all the warps in order while feeding them through the rigid heddle, one at a time. So be sure to wrap the warp threads around the cross dowels properly.
4. Begin zig-zagging around the dowels, until you come to the end of the guide string. Tie it to closest dowel. This will be the path for measuring all of the warps for each warp color bundle.

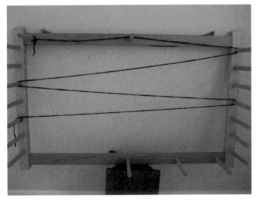

Warping board with guide string creating the path for the warp threads to follow. Notice the guide string has wrapped around the first dowel in the *cross section*.

Measuring Warp Threads on the Warping Board

Measuring the warp threads is conducted the same way for all three of the different models of tape looms. There are two methods to measure the warp threads on the warping board, with pros and cons for each method.

In Method A, each colored bundle of warps is measured and tied off separately. In Method B, the pattern draft is followed, cell-by-cell, working across from left to right, measuring each color needed in the sequence. Only one bundle of different colored warps is made.

I measure the warp threads using Method A, which I find easier to follow. Method B takes more time, in constantly referring to the draft. Method B has the benefit, though, of feeding the warp threads into the rigid heddle in an orderly fashion, once all the warps are measured.

Method A: Measuring the Warp Threads by Colored Bundles

1. Tie on the first colored warp thread to the top left dowel. Wind this thread through the *cross section* and, following the path of the guide string, around the rest of the needed dowels.

   Once at the end of the guide string, go around that dowel and following the same path, go up to the beginning top left dowel, wrapping around the dowels in the path. Continue until the total warps for that particular color have been measured.

   Warp Thread Number 1 goes from the top left dowel down to the bottom dowel. Warp Thread Number 2 goes from the bottom dowel up to the top left dowel. Each warp colored bundle is quite small, so simply count the number of threads needed, as you wrap them around the warping board.

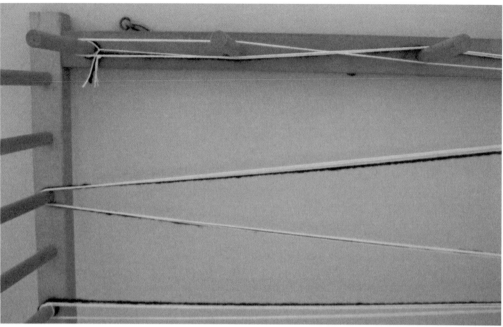

White warp threads tied around the guide string path, and back up to the top dowel. Guide string peeking behind the warps.

White warp threads having been chained up to top dowels. Ready to be pulled off the warping board and fed into the rigid heddle.

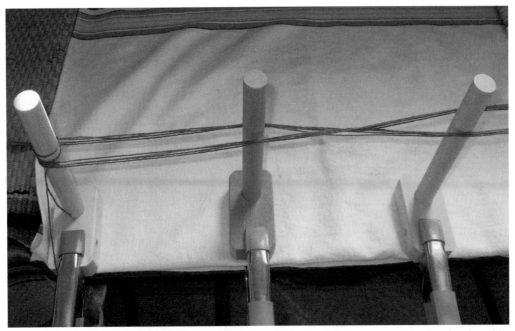

Close-up of measuring of warp threads with set of 4 pegs. Three of them are seen in this picture and the fourth would be to the right, measuring the total length of warp threads.

2. **Cross tie:** Tie off the *cross section*. Take a contrasting colored scrap thread and feed it through the four quadrants of the cross and tie loosely. Be careful not to tie the guide string into the cross tie. (I think every hand weaver has done that at least once!)

3. **Chain up:** Pull away the end of the warp bundle from the bottom dowel and circle around your wrist. Take your hand out of circle and grab the bundle above, pulling into the circle. Continue making a crochet chain up the warp bundle, to the cross section and pull remaining warp threads off the top dowel. (It is much simpler to actually do versus explain here!) See the bottom photo on page 124.

Method B: Measuring the Warp Threads Using the Peg Setup

If you don't have a warping board, the Peg Setup works well.

This method of measuring the warp threads has been used by numerous cultures for many centuries, usually by putting their pegs right into the ground. Lots of squatting, though!

- Attach four pegs to a table (easier than squatting on the ground) with clamps. It is a good idea to have the designated *cross section* close to the first peg, as on the warping board. The end peg, to the far right, should measure the length of the guide string (not showing in the photo).

Warping the Box Loom—Elizabeth's Way

Elizabeth Bertheaud, the director of the Ephrata Cloister in southeast Pennsylvania, shared with me her warping technique for the museum children's tape weaving classes. It is quite an ingenious idea, her version of a spool rack. She placed thirteen sewing spools, each wrapped with a measured amount of warp thread, over nails equally spaced and pounded into a 2-by-6 board. Elizabeth told me that thirteen warps were her standard number of threads. She proceeded to pull the warps off the spools, one at a time, feeding them directly into the rigid heddle of her box tape loom and continuing the warping process to the back of the loom.[1]

Warping the Tape Loom: Three Different Models

Warping the small tape loom is relatively easy compared to the lengthy process on larger types of handlooms. There are usually no more than 35 to 40 holes and slots for threading through the rigid heddle. After all of the colored warp bundles are measured, the next step is to "warp" the loom.

Putting the warp threads on the loom does require some concentration. As with warping any loom, it is a good idea to allow for warping the loom without any interruptions.

I will be discussing the warping process for the three models of tape looms—the paddle, the box, and the floor loom. The warping takes place from the front to the back of the loom. In Chapter 2, I laid out the basic design differences of

Grabbing all warp threads into one bundle, Elizabeth pulls the warp threads through the rigid heddle.

After tying on the warp threads to the roller, Elizabeth "beams up" or winds the warp threads on to the back roller. Warp threads travel from little "bobbins" of thread in front, through the heddle, to the roller at the back of the loom, where they are stored for weaving.

Elizabeth begins to weave tape. Notice the fish netter being used as the shuttle.

these three models of tape looms. Now, in the warping of these three looms, the differences will be more closely understood. The following instructions are for the box and paddle loom. See page 137 for floor or standing loom instructions, which are a little different.

The supplies needed to begin warping are the pattern draft, a pencil, a tape measure, scissors, and the colored warp bundles. Also, for pulling the warp threads through the heddle holes, you'll need a heddle hook; a small crochet hook, if it fits through the heddle holes; or a dental loop, which can be found at most pharmacies and works very well.

Feeding the Warp Threads through the Rigid Heddle

Define the middle of the rigid heddle and the left selvage. Begin by marking the middle of the

If working with a paddle loom, place the paddle between your legs, perpendicular to the weaving position, to begin the warping process.

heddle with a dot at the middle hole or slot. A tiny pencil mark is adequate. This mark can act as a counting guide when feeding the warps through the heddle. Then, divide the total number of warp threads in half, i.e., if there is a total of 20 warps, half of that would be 10. Starting at the middle mark, begin counting to the left, all of the holes and slots, until reaching the halved number. This will define the left selvage. Mark it with a scrap thread pulled through either the selvage hole or slot.

At this stage, it is important to follow the draft accurately, for warp color placement.

Feeding the Warp Threads into the Rigid Heddle by Colored Warp Bundles

Each colored warp bundle is fed into the rigid heddle separately, according to the draft. It is recommended to begin with the largest bundle of warps. That way, many holes and slots get filled and the smaller bundles are easier to feed in, toward the end of the process.

The Cross in Hand

Since there are not that many warp threads to be fed into the tape loom, keep the warp bundle in your hand, while feeding the warp threads into the rigid heddle. This method is relatively easy and quite comfortable.

Starting with the largest colored warp bundle, cut across the top of the bundle. Lay the *cross section* of the warp bundle in your hand, between your fingers, with the *cross* in the middle of the palm. When feeling brave enough, cut the *cross*

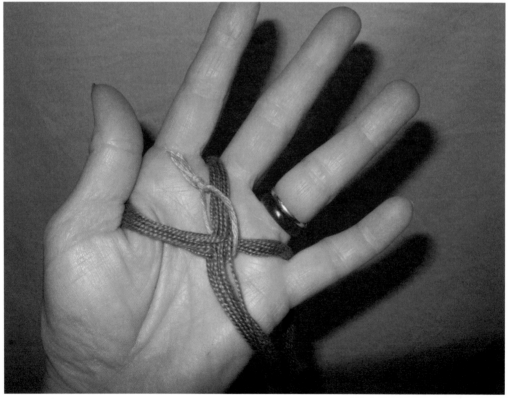

Close-up of cross in hand, ready to thread tape loom. Notice cross tie that separates the four quadrants.

tie. Hold your thumb down over the cross group to keep all those threads under control while feeding the warps into the heddle.

Take a deep breath. Now the real fun begins! Following one color in the draft, slowly pull off the TOP thread and feed it through the appropriate heddle hole or slot. Pull that warp thread behind the rigid heddle, for about a foot. (You don't want the warps to accidentally slide out of the heddle.)

Continuing to follow the draft, feed all the warps in *each colored warp bundle* through the heddle. Then pull all the warps together to the back of the loom. Line them up next to each other and tie an overhand knot, close to the warp ends.

Tying On / Beaming Up the Warp Threads

Paddle Loom:
Tying On the Warp Threads

Since the warp threads are not attached to a back beam, as on the box and floor loom, (One less step in the warping process!), the warp threads extending behind the paddle need to be tied to a pole, doorknob or something secure. I find it easier to tie the whole warp bundle to a strong leader cord and then tie the leader cord to a pole. That way there isn't the bulk when tying the warp knot at the pole.

With the paddle between your knees, in the weaving position, straighten out the warp threads in front of the paddle. Collecting them all under consistent tension, tie the ends into an overhand

Putting "The Cross" Warp Threads into Lease Sticks

If you feel that you are "all thumbs," there is an alternative way of managing the *cross section* of the warps. You can make your own lease sticks to hold the cross. Then your hands are free for feeding the warps into the heddle, and the lease sticks can be reused for future projects.

Take two pieces of strong cardboard (the back of a tablet works well) or slats of wood, 1" by 3" each, and make a hole in each end. Lay them side by side and tie string loosely through the holes on one end only. Open up the four quadrants of the *cross*, sliding the first two on top of the lease sticks, and the last two to the bottom. Then, tie the string loosely through the second set of holes of the cardboard end. Lay the warp *cross* and lease sticks on the table in front of you and cut the cross tie. As if in the hand, pull off the warps, one at a time, top warp thread first, and feed through the heddle, continuing as in the method above. The photo shows the warp threads fed into a floor tape loom.

Lease sticks are an alternative way of feeding warp threads into the rigid heddle of the tape loom.

knot. The entire length of warp threads need to be under tension when ready to weave, so adjust the chair and the paddle to a comfortable position. The paddle loom is now completely warped. Hurray! To begin weaving, see Chapter 6.

The Box Loom: Tying On and Beaming Up the Warp Threads

Box tape looms have two different styles of back beams at the back of the loom. They are important parts of the loom, for winding on and storing the warp threads. The one style is the roller. It is a simple wooden dowel, but involves more attention when tying on and beaming up the warp threads. The reel style of back beam appears more complicated, but is designed to make the step of tying on and "beaming up" an easy task.

The Roller: Tying On the Warp Threads

There are many traditional tape box and floor looms with a simple wooden roller in the back of the loom.

The warp bundle can be directly tied to the back roller, but has a tendency to slip. I have several suggestions to help with this issue.

- A leader cord, approximately 5" long, can be tied tightly around the roller. The warp bundle knot can be tied to this leader thread and wound around the roller. This alleviates any slipping around the roller. This has an added bonus in that it adds length to the warp at the end of weaving. The warp threads will spread out as they are wound around the roller
- A very small nail can be put into the middle of the roller. The warp bundle knot can simply be looped over that nail.
- Other traditional looms have a staple or knob set into the roller for the warp bundle knot to be looped over.

These examples demonstrate how the warp bundle knot can be simply placed over a nail or knob and the winding on of the warp can begin. This method does not take much time, compared to tying on every warp thread to the roller as has been suggested.

Leader cord tied to roller on box tape loom, with warp bundle knot looped through. Now ready to wind warp on to the roller.

Floor tape loom with wooden knob attached to roller. Bundle of measured warp threads, secured with overhand knot, could be looped over knob, to begin winding on warp threads to roller. *Collection of Landis Valley Village and Farm Museum.*

Metal staple inserted into middle of back roller on floor tape loom. A bundle of measured warp threads can be slipped through the staple and tied into overhand knot, to begin winding on warp threads to roller. *Collection of Landis Valley Village and Farm Museum, Pennsylvania Historical and Museum Commission.*

Small nail inserted into middle of back roller on floor tape loom. Warp bundle knot can simply be looped over nail and wound on to roller. *Collection of Landis Valley Village and Farm Museum, Pennsylvania Historical and Museum Commission.*

The Roller: Beaming Up the Warp Threads

Once the warp bundle is secured to the back roller, using the back ratchet, wind the warp threads around the roller in one complete turn. Stop and place two wooden slats around the knot, one on each side. (See the text box for the "spacer" explanation.) Even if using paper as the main spacer, I recommend starting with the two individual, thin spacers. They make for a smooth rolling around the overhand knot.

Holding the warp bundle in one hand, slowly wind on the warp, inserting a spacer after a few turns or if using paper, insert it snugly and it will continue to be wound around the roller, along with the warp.

Then, from the front of the rigid heddle, give the warp bundle a tug. This tightens the warps being wound around the roller. Wind on more warp, adding spacers. At the front, shake or comb out the warps and give them a tug. Keep repeating this sequence until the warp is almost wound on to the back roller.

Go to the front of the loom, comb out the remaining warp threads in front of the rigid heddle, and, under a little tension, tie them into an overhand knot. Make sure that all of the warps have the same amount of tension. Protecting the warp threads now, can save frustration later, if one might get too loose.

The warping process is complete and it's time to weave! Please see Chapter 6.

Lots of Roller Nails

I have seen some looms with a set of nails all across the back of the roller. The idea is to tie each warp thread to a nail or to an individual leader thread that is attached to each nail. Some weavers tie each warp thread directly to the roller (or reel peg). Much patience is required for all of those knots to be tied. Eleanor Bittle, for instance, explained to me that she does take the time to tie on each individual warp thread to the number of leader threads necessary for the project.

Decide for yourself which way you feel more comfortable tying on the warp.

The Reel: Tying On the Warp Threads

The reel is also a traditional style of back beam, but involves more crafting in the making of the loom. It definitely adds some dramatic flair to the appearance of the loom. There is less work involved when winding on the warp threads, though, which is a nice feature.

Simply tie the warp bundle knot to the *inside* wooden dowel of the reel and the "beaming up" step is ready to begin.

Close-up of overhand knot tied to *inside* dowel of reel, allowing winding of warp threads around outside of reel.

Spacers

When using a roller style of back beam, there is a need to periodically insert spacers to protect the warps from digging into each other as they are being tightly wound around the roller and to separate them. Traditionally, thin wooden slats were used, as shown in the photo. Eleanor Bittle, being very traditional, winds on individual rye straw around her warp threads, as she winds on her linen warp.

Contemporary tape weavers might wind on a length of grocery bag paper or, my favorite, thin strips of wallpaper. They both work well and are quite sturdy. They should be cut to a width that fits comfortably around the roller. But, not too wide that the paper rubs the frame of the loom and not too narrow that the warp threads can slide off the paper. If there is a lot of length to the paper spacer, simply wind up the excess and clip it together with a clothespin.

Floor tape loom has thin wooden slats periodically placed as spacers, lying against warp threads, protecting threads as wound around roller. *Collection of Landis Valley Village and Farm Museum, Pennsylvania Historical and Museum Commission.*

Strips of wallpaper work well as spacers to separate warp threads during "beaming up" process. Eva, author's cat, just had to help.

Eleanor Bittle has wound linen warp threads around roller of her tape loom. Rye straw is added periodically to protect warp threads from wrapping around each other.

In rye straw bundle, individual straw is seen quite strong and functions well as spacers for warp threads, wrapped around roller of tape loom.

The Reel: Beaming Up or Winding On the Warp Threads

After the warp is secured, holding the warp bundle in one hand, begin winding the warp bundle slowly around the reel, using the back ratchet. The warps do not need to be manually separated nor spaced out, as on the roller. The reel takes care of that. After a few complete turns, go to the front of the rigid heddle and give the warp bundle a tug, which tightens the warps being wound around the reel. Shake or comb out the warps and continue winding on the warps, giving a little tug from the front, periodically. Keep repeating this sequence until the warp is almost wound on to the back reel.

Go to the front of the loom, comb out the remaining warp threads in front of the rigid heddle, and, under a little tension, tie them into an overhand knot. Make sure that all of the warps have the same amount of tension. Protecting the warp threads now, can save frustration later.

The warping process is complete. You are ready to have fun weaving! Please see Chapter 6.

A "Reel" Confession

I was a little late in discovering the magic of the reel. When first learning about tape looms, my experience was with tape looms that had rollers on the back, not reels. So when I began warping box looms with reels, I would continue to wrap paper around the reel, as with the roller. So silly! The functionality of the reel had not sunk in and I was inadvertently doing much more work than necessary. We always remember the hard lessons, eh?

Reproduction box tape loom, hand built by Jonathan Seidel, showing warp threads being wound around reel.

The Floor Tape Loom

The floor, or standing, tape loom is somewhat different from the paddle and the box models of looms, in that it has legs, either three or four, and two rigid heddles that are attached to two floor treadles. That frees up the hands to weave the shuttle back and forth, without having to move the warps up and down. I consider my floor tape looms to be my production looms, allowing me to weave tape at a slightly faster pace.

Feeding the Warp Threads into the Rigid Heddles

Feeding the warp threads into a floor loom is conducted in the same way as with the other two models of looms. There is one exception, though. The floor loom has a set of *two* rigid heddles. Both of them should be lined up precisely, one behind the other. It's a good idea to tie the two heddles together, temporarily, making the warp easier to pass through both heddles at the same time. Having one of the above listed tools to pull the warp threads through both heddles at one time is advised.

Reproduction floor tape loom with warp threads fed through two rigid heddles, to back roller. Dave Hoffman hand crafted this tape loom.

Floor Loom Note

The warp bundle is tied on to the back roller or reel and "beamed up" in the same manner as the box loom. Then tie the front warp bundle to the front rollers, as described below.

Tying to the Front Rollers

Once the warp is completely wrapped around the roller or reel, go to the front of the loom for the last step. The design of the floor loom includes a tiny front roller and a cloth roller with a hole in

it. After straightening out the front warps, the warp bundle is slipped over the tiny front roller. Make sure the warps are in line and not lying on top of each other. Then, take the bundle back to the cloth roller with the hole. This is where the warps will be attached. Slide all of the warps through the hole, tying them into an overhand knot.

That will keep the warp threads tied to the loom.

Let the weaving begin!

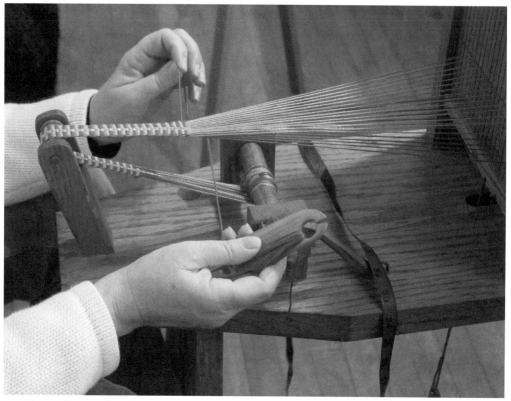

Reproduction floor tape loom has set of warp threads that have been slipped over tiny front roller and tied to cloth roller behind it, so tape weaving can begin.

6. Weaving on the Tape Loom

Now that the loom is all "warped," it is time to weave! Getting the tape loom prepared for weaving does take a little time. Surprisingly though, it becomes easier with every tape weaving project, as you become more comfortable with the process. And the same goes for the weaving of your tape. It weaves up quite quickly, after a little practice. Because the web is so narrow, passing the shuttle back and forth can feel somewhat awkward in the beginning. But soon you will be weaving lots of tape, for many colorful and interesting projects.

Shuttle lying inside traditional standing tape loom has an interesting shape, thin and flat for wrapping weft thread. Notice the rib pattern on handwoven tape. *Shuttle, Bequest of Henry Francis du Pont. Courtesy of Winterthur Museum.*

| Sisterly Tape | Tape Tale #6 |

On such a rainy afternoon, nine-year-old Emma takes a break from her chores out in the barn and runs into her family's log house. She is hoping to return to the tape loom and her weaving. She is so proud of the many yards that she and her older sisters have woven and wound onto the back roller on their standing tape loom. If she can finish weaving the tape today, they will be able to unwind the long narrow band, cut it from the loom, and examine the colorful pattern.

A little later, as the light fades from the Schrubb, or sitting room, and the evening sets in, Emma brings the tape loom closer to the oil lantern's brightly burning linen tape wick. She has just a few more inches to weave. Hearing her older sisters in the kitchen preparing the evening meal with her mother and her grossmutter, she listens to them telling one of their many family stories, and recalls the many hours she and her sisters shared in weaving this beautiful, long tape.

The Shuttle

Before the weaving can begin, the shuttle needs to be wrapped. A small, lightweight belt shuttle, no longer than 5", is a nice tool and is much easier to pass from one hand to another than a larger, more bulky shuttle. This is especially true when weaving on a box or paddle loom, where the hands are busy moving the warp up and down, as well.

A Beveled Edge

It is a good idea for the belt shuttle to have a thin, beveled edge on the one side. This is important for packing in the weft, giving the tape a clean and defined pattern.

I have seen tape weavers using a fish netter as a shuttle, and I've even observed them on displays at museums, next to a tape loom. This tool originally was used to make fish nets, hammocks, or the canopies on bedsteads. It can be used for weaving tape, but for a sharp pattern line, I recommend a belt shuttle with a beveled edge.

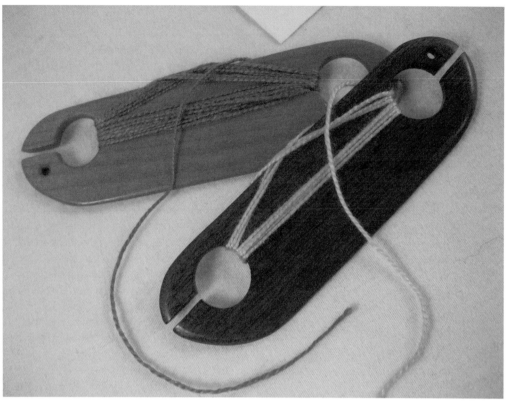

Two modern belt shuttles each have a beveled edge and weft wrapped in proper way, in a "figure 8," around top edge only. Hand crafted by Jonathan Seidel, tape loom maker.

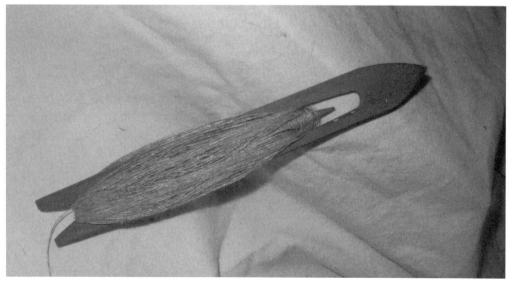

Fish netter has linen wrapped around both edges. Several images in this book show fish netters used as shuttles for different tape looms. I prefer to use a belt shuttle with a beveled edge on one side, to pack in weft thread as weaving takes place.

Wrapping the Weft on the Shuttle

Holding the shuttle in one hand, place the weft thread in the center of the shuttle, vertically, holding it down with your thumb. Begin wrapping your shuttle several times in the middle, from top to bottom. Begin the "figure 8" by *wrapping the side without the beveled edge,* from the back, out to the left, around the bottom, and up. You will notice the "X" forming on the left side of the shuttle as you wrap. Then wrap a few straight up and down threads. Continue wrapping on the side and in the middle of the shuttle. Don't get carried away and put on a huge amount of weft on the shuttle. It will just get caught in the sheds and rub against the warp threads. By wrapping the shuttle using the "figure 8" method, there will be lots of weft, and not too thick on the shuttle.

Inappropriate Shuttles

Many of us have been to fiber shows where a woodworker is selling weaving tools. When I examine the belt shuttles, if they do not have a sharp beveled edge, I won't buy one. A good woodworker can make a belt shuttle with a beveled edge almost as clean as a knife's edge.

The photo here is a crazy picture for a couple of reasons. This student inadvertently created the perfect "what not to do" example. A sleying hook, used with floor looms to feed the warp threads through the reed, is being used as a "shuttle" for this tape loom. Compare this to the two belt shuttles in the top photo on page 140. Also, notice the warp threads going through the rigid heddle, all on the right side. They should be directly in the middle of the heddle and be balanced on both sides. This is how we learn!

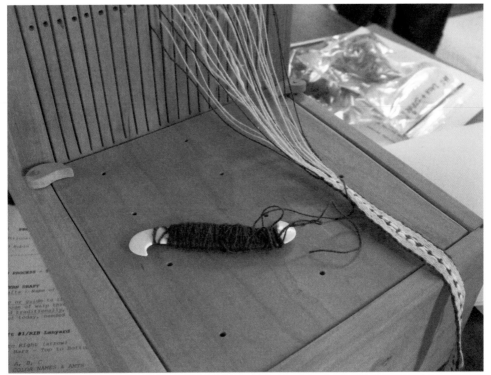

Reproduction English style box tape loom has sleying hook, tool for threading large floor looms, being used as shuttle. I definitely would not recommend using this tool in such a manner.

The Weaving Routine

The instructions in this section generally pertain to all three models of tape looms. Anything specific is noted and there is further information following this section, about the individual tape loom models.

Beginning to Weave

First row:

Holding the warp threads under good tension, approximately 2" from the initial knot, make an open shed and weave across, with a 3" tail hanging at the edge. Floor loom: Warps are tied to front of the loom and under good tension.

Second row:

Change sheds and tuck the tail midway in the warp threads, bringing it to the surface. In this same shed, throw the shuttle across and change sheds. Continue weaving.

Weaving Routine

- Open a shed, pulling on the front warp for good tension.
- Insert the shuttle midway into the shed, *beveled side to the front.*
- Beat (the previous row) with the shuttle in the same hand.
- Move the warp to neutral position (all the threads are lined up next to each other, with no open shed), locking in the shuttle so that it cannot move.
- With the same hand, grab the weft thread close to the weaving and give a little tug. This adjusts the selvage, keeping the width even.
- Switch hands and pull the shuttle gently across the row.
- Open the opposite shed and continue to repeat this weaving routine.

Weft Thread Choices

When choosing the weft color, there are two choices.

- Use the *same color* as the selvage warp thread. The weft thread will not be seen at all. It appears that traditionally, many tape weavers used the same colored weft as the selvage warp thread.

- Use a *contrasting color* from the selvage warp thread. This creates an accenting dot on the tape edges, which gives an interesting effect.

Two handwoven tapes have teal-colored weft threads, accenting selvages.

Passing the Shuttle Back and Forth

Begin either on the left or right side of the warp, in the "up" or "down" shed. It is easier to get into a directional routine when passing the shuttle back and forth. I usually begin by throwing the shuttle from left to right, in the "up shed" position. This helps me know where to throw the shuttle, as continuing to weave. I've had students who get confused, trying to remember which shed they are in. It may help to stick a note to the top of the rigid heddle with arrows identifying which direction the shuttle is to be thrown.

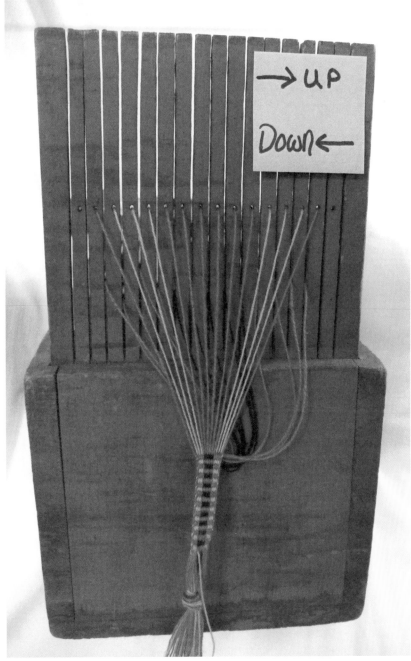

A note stuck on rigid heddle identifies which direction the shed should be in when weaving.

Measure the Width

Periodically measure the width of the woven tape, to make sure it is consistent. Sometimes "eyeballing" can be deceiving.

Advancing the Warp

As the tape continues to grow, the shuttle will get closer to the front of the rigid heddle. It is not a good idea to weave too close to the heddle. Trying to squeeze the shuttle into a tight set of warps could damage a warp thread, so it is advised to stop at about three inches from the heddle.

When more warp is needed in the weaving area, depending on the model of tape loom, the warp is pulled forward from the back of the loom to the front of the heddle.

On the *box and floor tape looms,* release the ratchet in the back of the loom and slowly pull more warp forward, stopping when there is about a foot of warp threads in front of the heddle. Adjust the ratchet and tighten the tension to continue weaving. This is called "advancing the warp."

If using a *paddle loom,* the weaver can move the chair forward to bring more warp threads to the front of the heddle or the warp can be untied at the back post and brought forward, tying the warp to the back post once the warp has been advanced.

Adding More Weft Thread or Splicing

Never tie a knot when the shuttle runs out of weft yarn. (That goes for any handwoven project.) Simply splice or overlap. Wrap the shuttle with more weft thread, including the "figure 8." In splicing, the "old" tail and the "new" tail are spliced together or overlap each other, *inside of the shed.*

The "old" tail is the end of the last weft. When coming to the end of a weft thread, weave the weft close to the selvage, within several warps from the edge, but not on the edge. Bring it to the top of the tape. Continuing in the *same shed* that the "old" tail is in, going in the *same direction,* pass the shuttle completely through the shed. Find the beginning of this new weft and bring it on top of the woven tape, about one half inch back from the "old tail" and again, not on the edge. The "new tail" is lying on top of the "old tail," inside of that same shed. Sort of magic, but it works beautifully!

Be sure not to pull out the new weft as you begin weaving again. The spliced area, where the "new" and the "old" weft are joined, will get packed down and remain snug as the weaving continues.

Trimming the Tails

It's a good idea to trim all the tails after the woven tape is off the loom, when they can be trimmed at the same time.

To trim, gently pull on the tail, hold the scissors snug to the woven tape and cut. Be careful not to cut into the actual weaving. Once the tails are trimmed, no one will know that the two weft threads had been spliced together. They have totally disappeared. For those tidy weavers that really want to trim their tails as they weave, do not trim the tails immediately after splicing the weft threads together. Weave several inches beyond that point, so that the tails won't slide out.

Joining a New Set of Warp Threads to the Loom

When starting another tape weaving, here is a timesaving tip for moving a new set of warp threads through the heddle a little quicker. Traditionally, professional weavers would do a larger version of this same technique on their wide barn looms. And weavers have continued ever since. Weaving does have its slow moments, so when one is shown how to speed up the process a little, most weavers are thrilled.

On any model of tape loom, though, this will only work for a rigid heddle with relatively large holes and if the new set of warp threads are not very thick. If that is the case, when one weaving project is finished and it is time to start another, there is an easy way to begin.

Rather than pulling off all of the warp threads through the heddle, from the previous project, and completely starting over, follow the new pattern draft and tie the measured warp threads for the new project to the former set of warps that are hanging off the front of the rigid heddle. Once all are tied on, gently pull all the warps, knots and all, through the heddle, to the back of the loom. This technique saves the time needed to feed each warp thread through a hole or a slot in the rigid heddle. Cut off the old warps and knots and tie the new warp bundle into an overhand knot. Attach the bundle to the back roller or reel, beam up this new set of warps and a new tape project is ready to begin.

Tape Loom Model Notes

The "Walking" Box Loom

While weaving, the tension on the warp threads is created by pulling on them in the front of the heddle. On a box loom, this can lead to the loom "walking" toward the weaver. There are several ways to alleviate this from happening. Traditionally, if the box loom was large enough, a brick could have been placed behind the heddle, in the box, as added weight.

Place a rubber mat under the loom as it is sitting on the table. Mats designed to keep a rug from slipping can be bought in a large sheet, which can be cut down to fit under the loom. In many cases, the loom will stay planted where it should be.

Hammer a small nail into the top of the back of the box loom. Tie a strong cord, or tape, to it and to a table leg or some other appropriate post. Then, position the loom, pulling it forward, creating the necessary warp tension.

There are some box looms built with a small hole in the back of the box, which can also be used for tying on a cord or tape itself to create better tension.

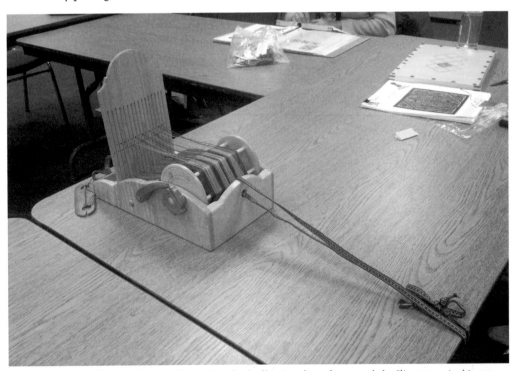

To prevent "walking" box tape loom, built in hole on back of box tape loom frame can help. Slip rope or, in this case, handwoven tape, through the hole and tie it to table leg. Notice two sets of heddle holes in the rigid heddle of reproduction model of box loom, hand crafted by Jonathan Seidel. Tape woven by Dee Lande. *Courtesy of Dee Lande.*

The New England Style Box Loom

For those weavers who have a New England style box loom, the weaving process is a little different, due to the built-in beater and the two sets of heddles. By having the beater as part of the tape loom, the purpose of the shuttle is simply to throw the weft across each shed. The beater does the work of tightly packing down the weft. Therefore, a different weaving routine would be in order, as well as for changing the two heddles by hand.

Weaving on a Floor Tape Loom

As mentioned earlier, the floor tape loom allows the weaver to have the hands free to focus on throwing the shuttle back and forth and beating the weft in place. It is very much like a larger floor loom, with two rigid heddles and two foot treadles to make the sheds. There is a rhythmic routine created by throwing the shuttle and opening the sheds with the feet.

The New England Style Floor Loom

The New England style floor tape loom is similar to the New England style box loom, in that it also has a built-in beater. This floor model has two sheds opened by two rigid heddles attached to the two foot treadles.

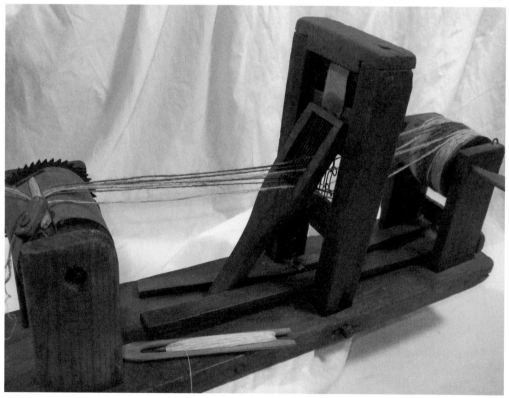

Traditional New England style box tape loom with built-in beater and two wire heddles. Canvas strap moves two heddles up and down. Linen warp and fish netter for shuttle. These fish netters are everywhere! Notice wooden wedge acting as brake mechanism in the back. *Collection of Eleanor Bittle, The Tape Lady ©.*

7. Contemporary Tape

Living on a farm during the American colonial period was about being resourceful and frugal, so the majority of the family tape was homemade. If there would be a little extra money, perhaps a farm wife would splurge on some store-bought tape for a special occasion. In our modern times, we have access to more consumer goods than we will ever use or need, including lots of inexpensive ribbon. Modern commercial ribbon costs about 50 cents for many yards. Very cheap! So why would anyone go to the trouble of weaving their own tape ribbon? One could ask the same thing about weaving one's own hand towel, knitting a winter cap, or creating any craft, for that matter.

Life is not about being a good consumer. Creating something with your own hands and talents is more about the journey, the process of making something yourself. It is about the feeling of empowerment, of knowing that you have built or made something with your own hands, of challenging yourself and accomplishing that goal. The rewards of self-creating mean so much more.

Local Amish of Today

Living in Lancaster, Pennsylvania, for many years, I've gotten to know some wonderful Amish people that live in the area. In their homes, the women do a lot of hand and machine sewing for their families. But, they buy their fabric, primarily wool and polyester, solid, plain colors, in the general store. Prints are too "fancy"! Local Amish women do not weave tape. The tape that is attached to their caps and bonnets has been commercially woven and store bought.

Several years ago, while visiting two older Amish sisters, I took one of my box tape looms along, to see if there would be any interest in weaving tape. I put it on their kitchen table and began demonstrating the weaving process. I explained how this was from *their* history, going back several hundreds of years, and how many farm families would make their own tape for all of their family needs. All the while, the one sister was making faces and shaking her head, "no." When asked what she thought of all of this, her reaction was, "That looks like too much work!" She wanted no part of my tape loom. Disappointing, but I respected her feelings. Silently, I thought of all of the hard, physical work that Amish women do every day for their families. But, alas, no tape weaving anymore.

Historical Museum Reenactors

Reenactors love their tape looms! I've conducted group classes just for docents, people who work in museums or other historical sites. They have a lot of interest in the history of tape, so that they can pass on the historical and traditional information to visitors. The box or paddle tape looms are so convenient to carry with them for demonstrating. If they wear an authentic colonial period outfit, docents can point out the tape that's holding up their own clothes. Museum visitors like to see handwoven tape that is used for numerous everyday purposes, as well as watching it being woven on a traditional loom.

Picnic Tape
Tape Tales #7

On a picnic with my relatives, after a yummy summer meal, I decided to relax and weave a little tape on my box tape loom. So I set it up on the picnic table and began weaving. Because it is small and portable, I often take it with me when flying to different events, or going on vacation. While my cousins and I were chatting, they began watching my bright purple, red, and green bamboo tape get longer and longer. They were quite impressed and each of them wanted to try weaving on my loom. When my four-year-old nephew came over to the picnic table, to my surprise, he took my shuttle and slowly attempted to weave some tape, with my help, of course. Slowly, "weaving" row by row, he had enough tape for a bookmark. I cut off his piece from the long tape and gave it to him. His face lit up into a huge smile as he proudly showed everyone at the picnic his own tape bookmark that he had woven himself.

Contemporary Patterns

Drafts are a wonderful tool for documenting and referencing when you want to weave a particular tape pattern. Chapter 4 shares a variety of traditional tape patterns woven during colonial times. Some of the pattern drafts that are shown in this chapter are taken from the traditional patterns and simply "jazzed up" to make them more contemporary. A common checkerboard pattern, warped in bright Christmas colors, maybe with a little glitzy metallic warp thread thrown in, can have a totally different look from the traditional "check" in blue and white bleached linen. Always remember how important color is to a tape pattern, especially contrasting colors.

If you find a draft that you like, play with it. You can expand the pattern, adding warps in different pattern sections. Or you can shrink it down to a narrower pattern. Graph paper makes a good record sheet. It is an easy way to draw out a draft, with the lines and cells already marked. Besides the draft, the rest of the page can be used for recording other project information, such as the date woven, tape length and width, and any comments on the outcome of the tape weaving project. Appendix 4 offers templates you can photocopy.

Contemporary Tape Ideas

There are a variety of uses for handwoven tape today. But as in early American days, when tape was woven for the quantity and *later* found its function, I have woven tape just because I liked a color combination, not planning it out for a certain use. So, play with color, and weave tape!

In this section of the book, a variety of ideas serve as a starting point for the many directions you, the reader, can take with your contemporary tape weaving. Many of these suggestions can make great gifts, for lots of occasions. A long woven tape can be cut apart into a selection of individual projects.

Group of tape bookmarks, woven in linen, cotton and hemp. Simple and easy-to-weave gifts for friends.

Miscellaneous

Tape bundles of different lengths make creative gifts in themselves. The recipient can cut apart the long tape and use it for a variety of projects. A few of the many possibilities:

- Garlands for a table, reflecting a theme or party colors
- Bookmarks
- Key bands
- Computer flash drive tabs for your computer
- Fix for a book that's falling apart

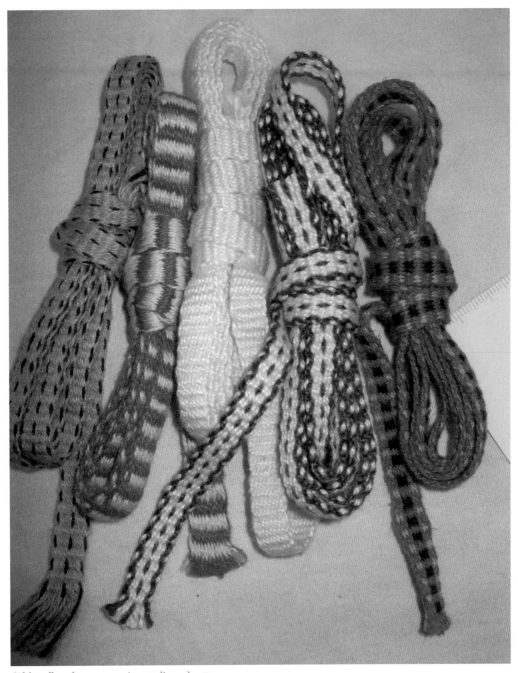

Gift bundles of tape, woven in cottolin and cotton.

Group of tape key bands, woven in cotton.

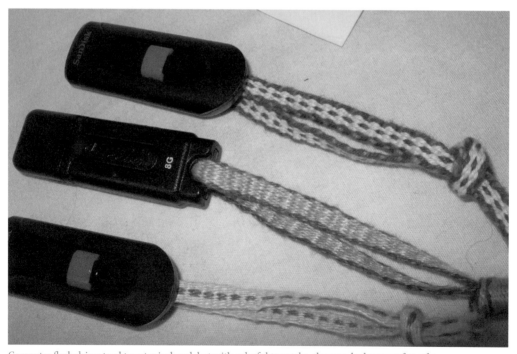

Computer flash drives tend to get misplaced, but with colorful tape tabs, they can be hung up for safety.

Example of tape to the rescue. My cookbook was falling apart from use. Tying a piece of handwoven cotton tape around it was a perfect solution.

Straps

- Dog leash
- Handbag or pouch strap

Bentley, neighbor's dog, wearing tape dog leash, hand woven in cotton. A wide loop of tape works for the handle.

Tape dog leash coming off box tape loom. Pattern is variation of traditional checkerboard pattern. Appeared in article by author in Sept./Oct. 2006 issue of *Handwoven Magazine.*

Handbag is complete with coordinated tape strap to finish the look. Abstract tape strap is woven in same churro wool as tapestry bag itself. Churro wool from rare breed of sheep of Navajo Nation. Tape strap and handbag woven by author.

Trim

- Hatband
- Clothing
- Flower pot or vase

- Jars of food items
- Cup, bowl, wrap silverware

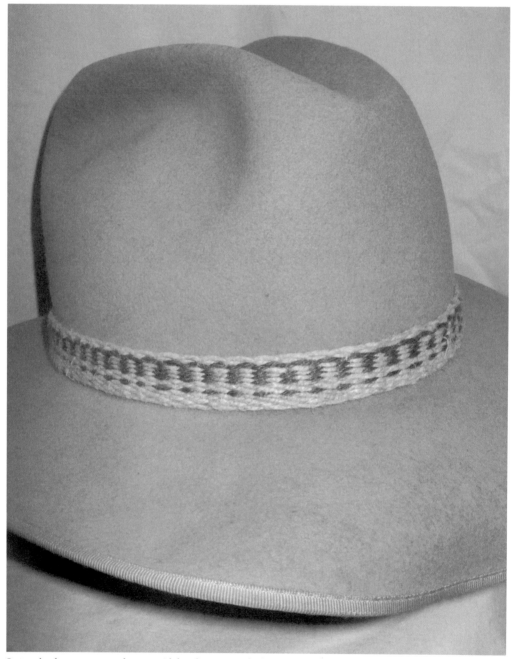

Stetson hat becomes so much more with handwoven tape hatband, especially when woven in hemp.

Little taste of linen tape, wrapped around small vase of lavender.

Ceramic vase wrapped with handwoven tape. Sample of variety of vases, glassware, and other vessels that can be accented with tape.

Any flowerpot can be decorated with tape for an added touch.

Food is a wonderful gift and when wrapped with handwoven tape, even better. These tapes, left to right, are of perle cotton, cottolin, carpet warp, and bundle is woven in hemp.

A special handmade pottery cup I use for my business cards, wrapped with linen and cotton tape.

Hanger Tabs
- Pot holder tab
- Kitchen tools
- Towel tab

Handmade cotton potholders with cotton tape tabs for hanging. The jar "could" be full of jam, with cotton cloth and tape decorating the top.

Kitchen tools with hanger tabs of cotton, cottolin, hemp and linen.

Hand weavers who weave up lots of kitchen hand towels can appreciate having their own tape tabs to sew on top of towel, for hanging. This cotton hand towel and tape tab woven by friend of author.

Decorative Hangings
- All kinds of wreaths
- Hanging tape bell
- Hanging heart

Wisteria wreath, made by my mother, decorated with homegrown sweet Annie plant (having a fragrance that you either really like, or don't!), decorated with long hemp tape.

Handwoven tape strap attached to cowbell. By weaving with thick weft, in this case, knit cotton, unique effect is created in the tape. Finished by wrapping warp threads and adding several beads.

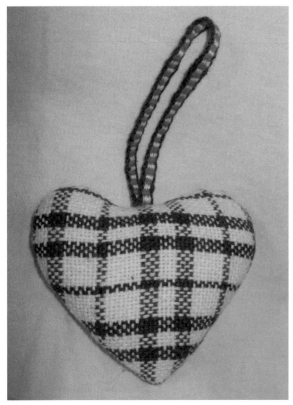

Stuffed cotton plaid heart with cottolin tape tab. Sweet decoration or gift. Hand woven by friend of author.

Ties

- Hair ribbon
- Assortment of bags
- Sachet bags
- Curtain ties
- Pillow or chair ties
- Gift packaging

Sachet filled with lavender, wrapped in fancy cloth, tied with cottolin tape.

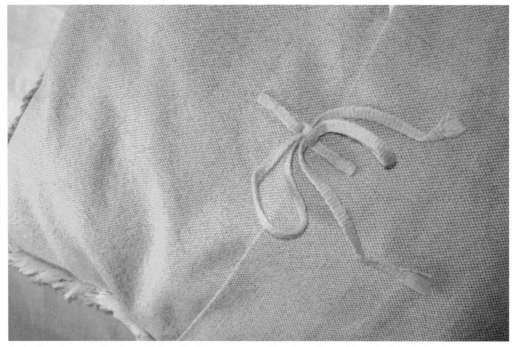

Back of handwoven pillow has added touch with woven tape pillow ties of linen. Woven by friend of author.

Any present can become extra special when wrapped with handwoven tape ribbon.

Accessories

- Bracelets. Once the bracelet length has been determined and cut, slide both tape ends through a bead with a relatively large hole, each going the opposite way. Finish with overhand knots and maybe a little fabric glue to smooth the ends. For the wider bands, the ends can be turned under and Velcro sewn over them.
- Belts
- Neck ties or necklaces
- Lanyards
- Jewelry tape pins

Many bracelets can be made from one long woven tape.

Tape belts, hand woven in natural hemp and connected by "D" belt buckle.

Dyed hemp belt with black buckle, easily adjusted to fit. Tape key bands also made from same long woven tape.

Sampling of my "tape ties," either tied around neck or long necklaces with accent bead and wrapping at bottom.

My lanyard for tape weaving class, woven in natural, blue and purple dyed hemp. Inside card has small amount of tape woven in natural and black hemp.

9/11 Memorial Flag Pin

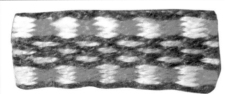

This American flag pin was designed by Eleanor Bittle, right after 9/11 happened, in 2001. This is a wonderful example of how an original tape pin can be made from any tape pattern. The tape is cut to size and glued to a piece of cardboard. The back of the tape is then glued to a jewelry pin. Eleanor sells them at a very reasonable price. You could make your own in different patterns and enjoy a whole collection of them.

Eleanor Bittle's 9/11 memorial pin, hand woven in linen.

Interesting "Add Ons" for Your Tape

Garlands on a table, for example, can feature "add ons" like these which really add interest to the tape.

- Cinnamon sticks, woven in. (See the photos on pages 180 and 181.)
- Reeds or other small stick-type objects, woven into the warp.
- Small bells, sewn on to the tape, after woven and off the loom. (See the photos on pages 180 through 183.)

SAMPLE TAPE PATTERN DRAFTS AND CHARTS

Next are some sample pattern drafts and charts to give you ideas for your own modern tape patterns. It's fun to play with a pattern and ask yourself, "What if I change these colors around a bit? What new pattern can I create?" Ideas can come from anywhere. Visualize your idea as tape, put it into draft form, and weave!

Watermelon Tape Pattern

Fiber: cotton carpet warp
Total Warps: 32
Color Code:
Green (G) – 8
Tan (T) – 6
Pink (P) – 16
Black (B) – 2

Neighbor's garden art inspired pattern for "watermelon" tape, complete with seeds, woven in cotton carpet warp.

Warp Color Draft ⟶

HOLE	G		G		T		T		P		B		P		P		P		P		P		P		P		T		G		G
SLOT		G		G		T		P		P		P		P		P		P		B		P		T		T		G		G

Tape Pattern Chart

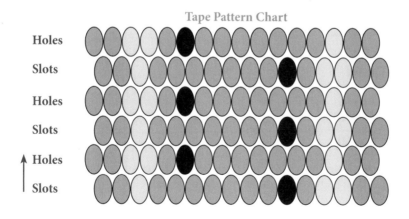

Yoga Mat Tape Pattern

Fiber: 5/2 perle cotton
Total Warps: 27
Color Code:
Blue (B) – 16
White (W) – 6
Tan (T) – 5

Yoga mats sometimes want to unwind, so tape ties keep them in place.

Warp Color Draft ⟶

HOLE	B		W		W		W		B		B		B		B		B		B		W		W		W		B
SLOT		B		B		B		B		T		T		T		T		T		B		B		B		B	

•

Tape Pattern Chart

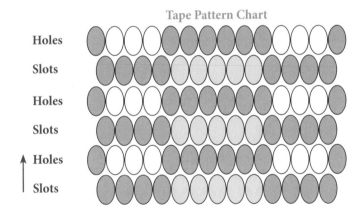

Holes

Slots

Holes

Slots

↑ Holes

| Slots

Holiday Tape Ideas and Pattern Drafts

When weaving holiday tape, think about the symbolic colors associated with that particular holiday. Fourth of July means "red, white, and blue." Thanksgiving usually means shades of gold, brown, green, and orange. Wreaths of evergreens can have tape wrapped into them for a wonderful color theme. Try making bookmarks with a holiday's theme colors, or wrap holiday gifts with tape. There are so many old and new holidays to explore these days. I hope these holiday tape examples will get your creative juices flowing.

St. Valentine's Day Tape Pattern

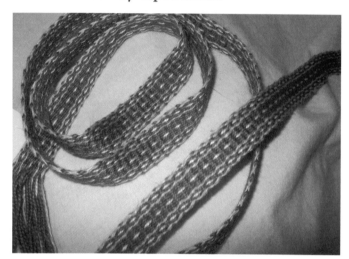

Fiber: 5/2 perle cotton
Total Warps: 31
Color Code:
Pink (P) – 8
Red (R) – 20
White (W) – 3

Warp Color Draft ⟶

HOLE	P		R		W		R		P		R		R		R		R		R		R		P		R		W		R		P
SLOT		P		R		R		P		R		R		R		W		R		R		R		P		R		R		P	

•

Tape Pattern Chart

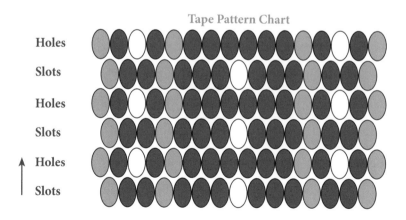

Holes
Slots
Holes
Slots
↑ Holes
| Slots

St. Patrick's Day Tape Pattern

Fiber: 3/2 perle cotton
Total Warps: 27
Color Code:
Green (G) – 15
White (W) – 12

Warp Color Draft ⟶

HOLE	G		G		G		W		G		G		W		W		G		G		W		G		G		G
SLOT		G		G		W		W		W		W		G		W		W		W		W		G		G	

Tape Pattern Chart

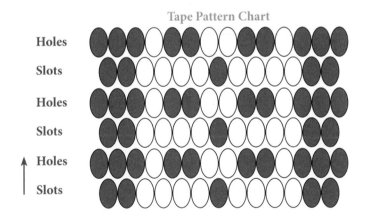

Holes

Slots

Holes

Slots

↑ Holes

Slots

Cinco de Mayo Tape Pattern

Fiber: 3/2 perle cotton
Total Warps: 27
Color Code:
Red (R) – 12
White (W) – 8
Green (G) – 7

Warp Color Draft →

HOLE	R		R		W		G		W		R		R		R		R		W		G		W		R		R
SLOT		R		W		G		G		W		R		G		R		W		G		G		W		R	

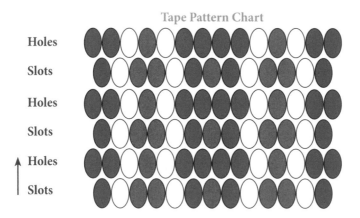

Tape Pattern Chart

Holes
Slots
Holes
Slots
Holes
Slots

Fourth of July Tape Pattern

Fiber: 5/2 perle cotton
Total Warps: 31
Color Code:
Red (R) – 10
Blue (B) – 10
White (W) – 11

Warp Color Draft ⟶

HOLE	R		R		R		R		R		W		W		W		W		W		B		B		B		B		B		B
SLOT		R		R		R		R		R		W		W		W		W		W		B		W		B		B		B	

•

Tape Pattern Chart

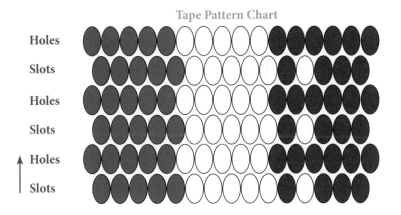

Holes

Slots

Holes

Slots

↑ Holes

| Slots

Halloween Tape Pattern

Fiber: 5/2 perle cotton
Total Warps: 27
Color Code:
Orange (O) – 9
Black (B) – 18

Warp Color Draft ⟶

HOLE	B		O		B		B		B		B		B		B		B		B		B		B		O		B
SLOT		B		B		O		O		O		B		O		B		O		O		O		B		B	

•

Tape Pattern Chart

Holes

Slots

Holes

Slots

↑ Holes

| Slots

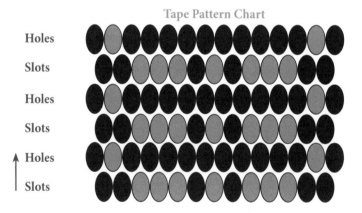

Thanksgiving Day Tape Pattern

Fiber: 5/2 perle cotton
Total Warps: 33
Color Code:
Black (Bl) – 8
Brown (B) – 8
Gold (G) – 7
Orange (O) – 6
Green (Gn) – 4

Warp Color Draft ⟶

HOLE	BL		B		B		BL		BL		B		GN		GN		G		GN		GN		B		BL		BL		B		B		BL
SLOT		BL		G		G		G		B		O		O		O		O		O		O		B		G		G		G		BL	

•

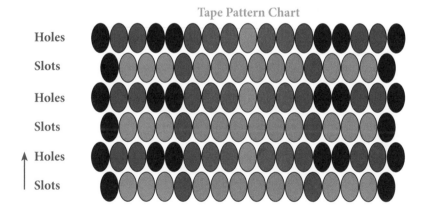

Tape Pattern Chart

Holes
Slots
Holes
Slots
↑ Holes
  Slots

Christmas Ideas

Christmas is a holiday of many decorations. Colorful Christmas tape really puts you in the spirit of the holiday and can be wrapped around so many things. So before the Christmas holiday, I weave lots of holiday tape to wrap it all up brightly. Here are some festive tape ideas to have fun with.

- *Christmas bookmarks.* Holiday bookmarks make great little gifts to add as last minute presents. Or, they can be a bonus gift, inserted into the top of the gift wrapping ribbon. Weave a long red and green garland, maybe adding a few threads of metallic gold for sparkle. Cut apart for many colorful bookmarks. Suggested directions are in the Finishing Tape section of this chapter.
- *Christmas wreaths.* These charming little fleece wreaths are made with white fleece from a local sheep. Wound around wire, the fleece is

tucked in, with the Christmas tape wrapped over the fleece.

Wreaths come in all sizes. And there are all of the holiday evergreens and holly with berries to decorate them with. So make ho! ho! with lots of holiday wreaths.

- *Tree ornaments.* Weave cinnamon sticks into a tape as you are weaving, to create Christmas trees. Cut the different lengths beforehand, from short to long "branches." Begin with the longest "branch," to the shortest. With a long warp on the loom, a number of trees can be woven at one time. While the woven tree is on the loom, wrap the top and bottom of the tree warp ends to hold it all in place. The trees can be cut apart once off the loom. A bell could be hand sewn to the top, as the star. Another idea is to hang the whole set of *vertical* Christmas trees as a festive wall decoration.

Christmas bookmarks make great stocking stuffers. Very thin Christmas tape woven by friend of author.

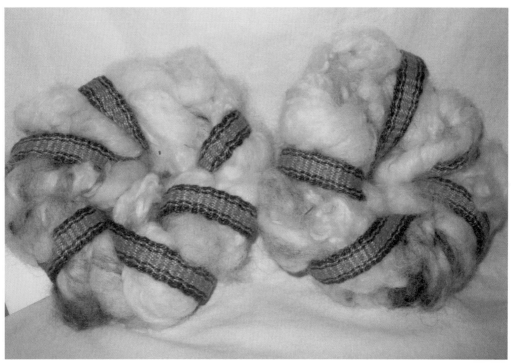

Wooly Christmas wreaths, wrapped in festive tape.

When I was living in Arizona, leftover agave fiber from other weaving projects made sweet holiday wreaths.

Festive holiday wreath made from wisteria and evergreens. Wrapped with handwoven tape garlands of red and green cotton and metallic gold. Bells added for little extra texture.

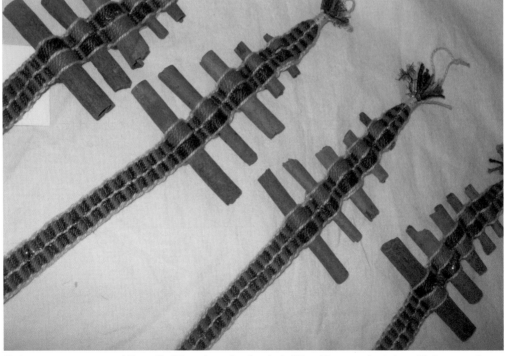

Christmas tree ornaments add lots of holiday color and make nice holiday gifts, or can be tied to a Christmas package as a bonus gift. Woven in red, green, and gold perle cotton, with touch of novelty red thread. Cinammon sticks turn tape into Christmas trees.

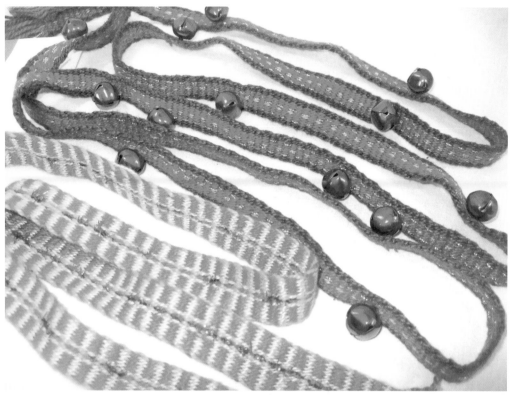

Decorative garlands.

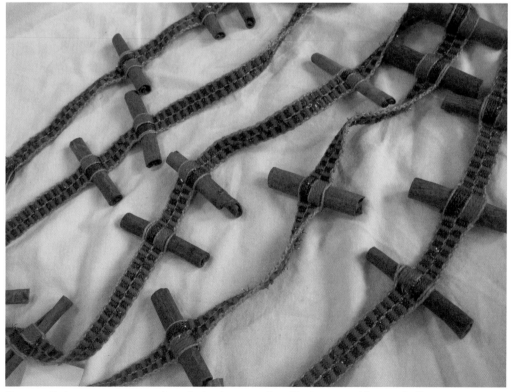

The same Christmas tape pattern as shown in the photo opposite, with cinnamon sticks sporadically woven in.

Christmas tree, wrapped with garlands of decorative tapes.

Christmas tape with bells, wrapped around gift box, adds a special and personal touch.

- *Christmas tape garlands.* Holiday garlands can be draped around a table for a festive accent, along with candles, Christmas balls and evergreens. Wrap your Christmas garlands around a stair banister, mirror, or doorway. Red, green, or gold bells can be hand sewn on to tape garland, on one or both sides. Weaving cinnamon sticks into the tape, periodically, creates instant cheer. Or, weave small candy canes into the tape, the same way as the cinnamon sticks. Children could have fun pulling them out and new candy canes could be reinserted later.
- *Christmas tape for the tree.* A friend made several very long tape garlands with cinnamon sticks woven in periodically and wrapped them around her Christmas tree. Even a small, artificial tree looks "all decked out" with Christmas tape on it.
- *Christmas gift boxes with handwoven tape ribbon.* Wrap lots of gifts with your holiday

tape, maybe with a group of bells in the warp fringe.
- *Displays of tape in glasses, jars, vases, or bowls.* Or, glue holiday tape to a variety of items for a festive feel. Christmas tape tabs can be used to hang a variety of decorations, as well.
- *Tape bows with mistletoe.* A bunch of mistletoe wrapped with Christmas tape can be hung (for that special kiss!) or glue a pin back to the back of the tape bow for a romantic Christmas interlude.

Tape for Special Occasions

Life gives us many reasons to mark special occasions, some happy, and others that are not so happy. Whatever the special occasion, handwoven tape is a wonderful "visual" in decorating for the event. And when your guests ask where you got it, you can tell them that *you made it!*

Before an event, the weaving of a long tape can be therapeutic for the tape weaver. It can be a reflective time, thinking of the reasons for that special occasion. Once off the loom, the tape can be cut apart for little memory gifts.

Receiving a personal tape bookmark as a small symbol of a special event can be a nice gesture. The tape could be placed in a card with some encouraging words or a small tag could be attached to the tape, with the title and date of the event. Tape can be a sweet way to remember that special day, a physical remembrance to hold (and use in a book). One can look back at the memories of that time together, with special people.

- Baby shower
- Birthday
- Funeral
- Baptism
- Retirement party
- Wedding shower or reception. To prepare for my own wedding reception, a number of years ago, I wove several long white mercerized cotton tapes, in a checkerboard pattern. I added a few threads of metallic glitz into the warp. They were then cut apart in eight inch sections and fringed. At the reception, I placed them into a fancy basket and all of the guests were asked to take one home with them as a little memento of their special time, a wedding

tape that bound friends and relatives together. Little white pearls could be an added touch, to the bottom of longer tape fringe as well.

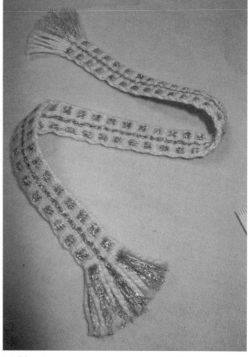

Wedding tape, given to guests at my wedding reception as a way to remember the special day.

A Good Friend's Request

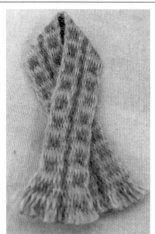

I received an unusual, but very poignant, request some time ago. A friend asked if I would weave some special tape. Her sister had just died from breast cancer and my friend had thought of the "pink ribbon" symbol. I gladly accepted the weaving project, and went one step further in the color theme; I decided to weave this special pink tape with a touch of green, since my friend's sister was very proud of being Irish.

The long tape was woven and cut apart into small sections, with a little fringe on each end. Once the small tapes were folded into the special breast cancer symbol, a tiny pin back was glued to each one. My friend gave these small gestures of love to family and friends, as a symbolic way of remembering her sister. I felt deeply honored to have played a small part during a bittersweet moment.

Poignant remembrance of a friend's loved one, in celebration of her life.

Supplemental Warp Threads

Supplemental warp threads are a way of adding another dimension to a tape, giving it a more textural look. By adding several extra, supplemental warp threads to the original set of warps, more color can be included to the original tape pattern.

Choose from one to several additional warp threads to be added to the whole warp. Using thicker yarn, such as cotton chenille, as the supplemental warp, makes the tape really "pop." Make sure the extra warps are strong enough to be added, though.

I have woven and sold handbags using the supplemental warp technique for a tape strap. It gives a cohesive look to the handbag, by tying in the color theme, from the handbag to the strap.

Supplemental warp threads can change the whole appearance of woven tape, creating more interest.

Cotton chenille handwoven handbag, with supplemental warp technique applied to woven strap. Woven by author.

Tape strap hand woven in supplemental warp technique. Antique button attached. Cotton chenille handbag woven by author.

Warping the Tape Loom with Supplemental Warp Threads

Extra warp threads can be added after the regular warp has been put on the loom, perhaps as an afterthought. Decide where you want them to be added, maybe randomly. From the front of the rigid heddle, feed them through either slots or holes, or both, on top of the regular warps. At the back of the loom, wind each of them around a weight of some kind. I use old film canisters with coins inside. That way I can adjust the weight needed. Just let the extra warp threads and the weights hang off the back of the loom. The "supps" will move up and down as part of the regular sheds. As the warp is advanced, you will need to unwind the extra threads in the back of the loom and adjust them.

Supplemental warps can be written into the pattern draft by choosing where you want them and adding their code letters in the particular cells of the draft. By planning them as part of the pattern draft, they will be tied to the roller or reel with the rest of the warp threads, and weights won't be necessary.

Contemporary Tape Fringe

There are numerous decorative ideas to explore in the making of tape fringe today. Different lengths of side or selvage fringe can be made, even adding beads for interest. I encourage you to go

to a fabric store and observe the enormous variety of commercial tape "trim" that is available. Get some ideas, and then play and weave fringe on your own tape loom.

As mentioned in Chapter 4, the tape acts as the "header" or cloth base for the fringe to hang off. Any tape pattern can become side tape fringe. Two shuttles are used for this fringe technique. One shuttle will hold the thicker fringe weft. This should be either one thick weft thread or several weft threads, wound together on the shuttle. The second shuttle will hold the "binder" thread, usually a much thinner weft thread.

Prepare a cardboard spacer, as wide as the intended fringe weft and approximately six inches in length. Insert it vertically next to the warp threads, once the weaving begins, and move it up as the weaving proceeds. When weaving with the two shuttles, the fringe weft will go around the vertical spacer and the binder thread will not.

Begin by weaving a few rows with the binder thread. In the last row of the binder thread, *in the same shed,* weave a row of fringe weft, going *in the same direction.* Change the shed and beat firmly. Weave a row of binder thread. Placing the spacer vertically next to the selvage, wrap the fringe weft around the spacer and through *the same shed* as the binder thread. Repeat this routine for the length of the side fringe desired.

Eleanor Bittle's reproduction linen fringe (see page 114 in Chapter 4) was woven on a standing, floor tape loom. The weaver has more control over the fringe making than on a box or paddle tape loom since the hands are free to maneuver the fringe making. Side fringe can be made on the box or paddle loom, but it is a slower process. Sarah Mifflin's famous picture depicts her weaving side fringe on a box loom. (See page 16.)

"Binder" Weft Thread Woven into Tape Fringe

The binder weft thread is woven into the tape header in order to keep the tape from unraveling into the fringe. As we saw in Chapter 4, many coverlets did not use the binder thread. It might be a more modern, as well as practical, idea. When weaving tape fringe, I suggest experimenting with and without the binder weft thread. Usually the binder thread is very thin, sometimes as thin as sewing thread. If you choose the same color as the selvage warp, the binder will not show at the edges.

Tape side fringe on left is unraveling; no binder thread woven across to hold warp threads in place. Tape side fringe on right shows use of cardboard spacer. Woven with two shuttles, using thick weft wool as fringe and thin binder thread; no unraveling.

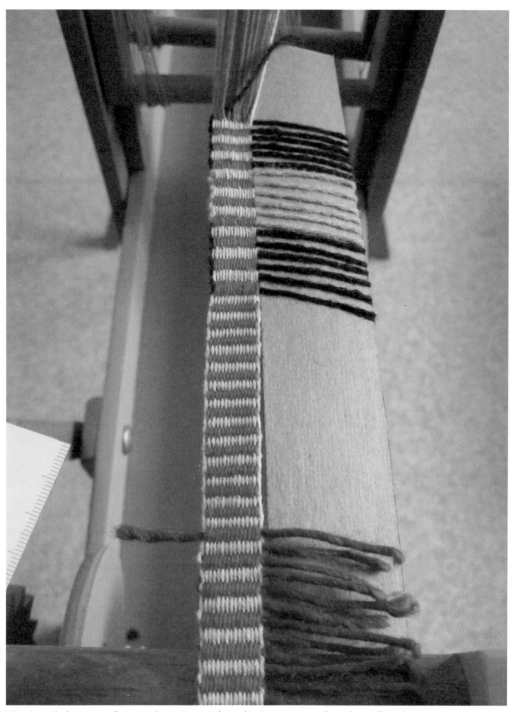

Weaving side fringe on a floor tape loom. Bottom fringe has been cut away from the cardboard spacer.

Wool tape fringe being woven on box tape loom by Gay McGeary. Two wool warps on the far right are for weft to wrap around, creating fringe. They will be discarded when the weaving is completed, and fringe will be cut. Notice two shuttles, one for the thick wool fringe weft and one for the thin binder weft, to keep it from slipping into fringe area. *Courtesy of Gay McGeary.*

Tubular Tape or Cordage

Tubular tape weaving or cordage is an interesting alternative to "flat" tape weaving. By throwing the shuttle in a slightly different manner, a circular cord is formed. The thickness of the cordage depends on the warp thread size and the amount of warp threads. Cordage can be used as a drawstring, trim, or for many other tape projects.

Begin by warping any type of tape loom. Any pattern may be used with different color combinations for interesting effects. I recommend weaving an inch of regular flat tape to start. This sets up the warp threads for the cordage. (It can be cut away when finished, if you do not want it.)

After the initial inch of regular tape weaving, in the next shed, weave across, from left to right (or right to left). Either direction works, but be consistent in repeating the direction that the shuttle is thrown.

Change sheds and bring the shuttle below the warps and up to left side. Throw the shuttle through the shed, to the right, pulling the weft tightly. This allows the selvages to meet, creating the curve of the cord. Repeat.

This manner of weaving can seem a little disconcerting at first, but with practice, it will feel more comfortable and can be an interesting technique. Try weaving a length of flat tape, then cord, flat tape, cord, for another unique look. In her book *Inkle,* Evelyn Neher goes one step further, weaving a length of flat tape, then cord, continuing as before, but then alternating the direction of the shuttle for the cord weaving, after each section of flat tape.[1] There is room for lots of experimenting with this weaving technique. See page 114 for Eleanor Bittle's examples.

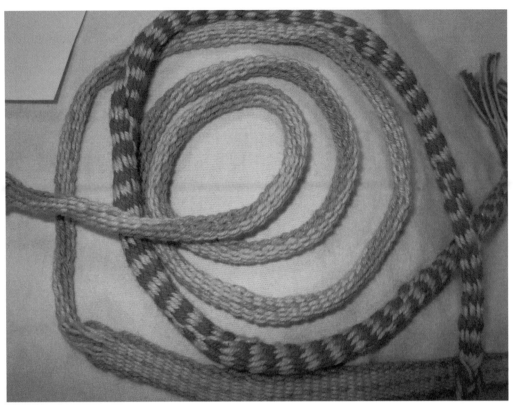

Tubular cordage handwoven on tape loom by the author.

Contemporary Tape Finishing and Storing

Finishing choices for tape ends depend on the purpose of the tape. Pre-planning and measuring may be needed so that the warp threads will be long enough, depending on the project. Beads, tassels, feathers, or bells are just a few ideas to add to the warp ends.

Tape End Fringe

For a tape with fringe on each end, simply cut from the loom, *unweaving* several rows to the length of fringe desired. The weft tails at the ends of the tape can be secured by needle weaving the tails into several of the previous rows at each end, with a tapestry needle. This type of needle has a big "eye" for the weft to go through easily and keeps the tape nice and tight at the ends.

Several bookmarks can be made from one long length of tape once the tape has been cut off the loom. Measure each bookmark length, allowing room for fringe and cut them all apart. Simply unweave several rows, using a tapestry needle to make fringe on each end. Again, needle weave in the weft tails, if desired.

Making End Fringe on the Loom, Using Cardboard Slats

There is another way of making numerous bookmarks or other projects, from one long tape. Fringe can be made for each, using cardboard slats that are inserted in between each bookmark, as you are weaving. Prepare the cardboard slats beforehand, by measuring them wider than the width of the tape, so the warps do not slide off. Decide on the length of the fringe for each bookmark and measure the cardboard slat accordingly. For one-inch-long fringe, the slat should be twice as long, two inches, one inch for the end of one bookmark and one inch for the beginning of the next bookmark. Weft tails can be needle woven into the previous row, while still on the loom. Once the whole tape is woven and cut off the loom, cut the warps in the middle of each cardboard slat, top and bottom, to separate the bookmarks that now will include their fringed ends.

Twisted Fringe
For a fancier fringe finish for your tape, try the fringe twister tool that makes quick and uniform fringe. This technique is only for a group of long, loose warp threads. It is made by Leclerc and is sold at most retail yarn shops. Tape does not have a lot of warp ends, but it is still fun to play with twisted fringe. The twist is created by twisting two small groups of warp threads in one direction. Then letting them spin together, in the opposite direction, where the final twist is created. Tie an overhand knot and the twist will remain in place. Since these are such small groups of warps, you can also make the twists with your hands just as easily as using the twister tool.

To finish tape ends, a fringe twister is good tool.

Tie Overhand Knots
There needs to be some length of loose warp threads in order to make the knot, but it is a quick finishing technique.

Braiding the Ends of the Tape
As described in Chapter 4 with historical tape, this technique is a great way to extend the length of a tape. Cut off the warps at the knot behind the rigid heddle and pull the long warps through the front heddle and out of the loom. Once off the loom, braid the leftover warp threads and tie an overhand knot.

Hemmed Tape Ends
Tuck the trimmed warp ends under at each end, rolling in slightly. Hand or machine stitch securely.

Machine Stitch
A quick way to secure the tape ends is on a sewing machine, simply sewing across the tape. You may want to use invisible thread, so the stitches don't show too much. Add a little fringe on each end and trim.

Storing Your Woven Tape
Storage of your tape is the same as centuries ago. Historically, Pennsylvania German families would store their family bundles of tape in their handmade rye straw baskets. Today, you can make your own storage basket or pick up a nice one at most re-use-it shops. See page 115 in Chapter 4 for more detailed information. Tape can be stored easily in bundles, balls, or tape holders and simply cut off, when needed.

Braided tape ends of different widths, depending on amount or thickness of warp threads. Bottom to top: tape of Tencel, linen, cotton carpet warp, linen, and two of perle cotton.

Examples of different tape finishing techniques. Bottom to top: fringe, overhand knot, hemmed and twisted fringe.

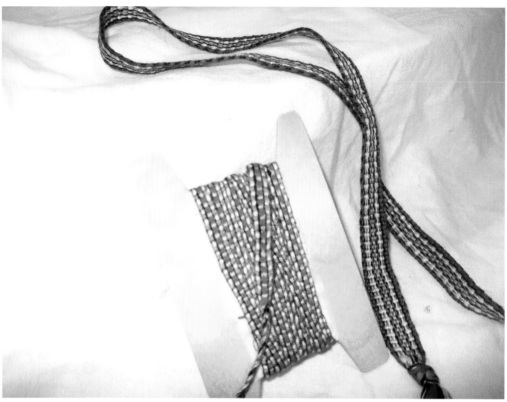

Handmade cardboard tape winder or holder, to collect length of tape, made by Eleanor Bittle. Notice the contemporary silk tape she wove in contemporary patterns.

Children's Tape Weaving

Tape weaving is a gentle way to share some American history with children. In the early American homes, much of the tape was most likely woven by the children. It was one of their ways of participating in the family household, helping with the many tasks of the day. The tape that they wove could be shared by all of the family members, for uses from clothing ties to tying off a section of a garden. By describing this American history, today's children, and parents, may be able to relate to the colonial concept of working together for the family.

The tape loom is a great way to introduce a child into the world of hand weaving. It is a small loom, so it is not too intimidating. Weaving tape can lead children into playing with color and even a little designing. Weaving their own bookmark can give a child a feeling of accomplishment and perhaps the desire to venture into other types of weaving.

Chris Yovino took one of my tape weaving classes for museum docents a number of years ago. Here is her story of the ties that bind students and tape looms at Hagley Museum, in Wilmington, Delaware.

"When I took Susan's tape loom weaving class, I knew tape weaving would be a perfect activity to use where I work at the Hagley Museum. We could use it at summer camps and at other museum events. It was perfect except for one thing. Where would we get looms? Using a plan my friend found in *Early American Life,* my friend's retired father made us three looms for the museum. Then he made one for my friend and one for me! They are always popular with both adults and children. We have used them every summer since they were made, eight years ago."[2]

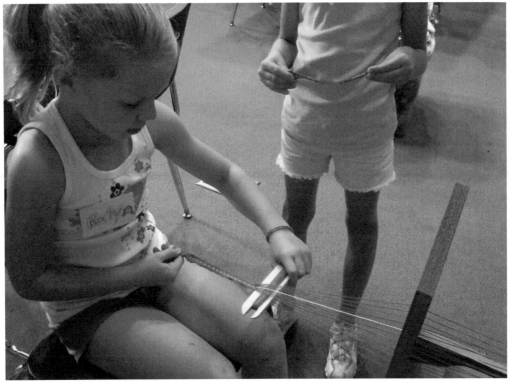

Summer camp at Hagley Museum, Wilmington, DE. Children learned to weave tape quite quickly and really enjoyed their experience. *Courtesy of Chris Yovino.*

Young summer camper at Hagley Museum weaving lots of good-looking tape. *Courtesy of Chris Yovino.*

Children weaving their tape at Hagley Museum summer camp, while others wait their turn. *Courtesy of Chris Yovino.*

The real tape "tail," belonging to author's cat, Eva, a rescue from Hurricane Katrina. She loves to pose for pictures!

Conclusion

The handwoven tape weaving journey, from its early American days to the tape weaving of today, is an extensive one. Today, in our modern world, tape is not a necessity for our clothing ties or for carrying our satchels to market, but for the simple, quiet pleasure of weaving these long bands of colorful tape, for our woven projects. May your tape weaving journey continue and may your ties be bound in joy.

Appendix 1

Contemporary Threads for Tape

Unless you are very skilled in your hand spinning, I recommend buying commercial thread for the tape warp threads. It needs to be smooth and strong and is much easier to buy it, with so many colors to choose from.

The following are available from most retailers.

Linen
14/2 or 16/2 line linen (2,400 yd./lb.)

Cottolin
8/2, 60% cotton/40% linen (3,360 yd./lb.)
8/2, 50% cotton/50% linen

Hemp
100 g (3½ oz.)

Cotton
Perle cotton, a mercerized cotton
3/2 (1,260 yd./lb.) and 5/2 (2,100 yd./lb.)
Cotton carpet warp—cheap, strong, lots of color choices
8/4 (1,680 yd./lb.)

Wool
Thin, smooth, and strong

Tensel
Thin, shiny, and silky, 8/2 (3,360 yd./lb.)

Rayon
Thin, shiny, and silky

Appendix 2

Resources on Tape, Tape Looms, and Coverlets

Tape Looms

"A Warp-Faced Dog Leash Woven on a Tape Loom," Susan Weaver, *Handwoven Magazine*, Sept./Oct. 2006.

Box tape loom designed by Susan Weaver and Chris Erickson
Warp Seed Studio's Facebook page

Eleanor Bittle (handmade cardboard looms)
610-367-0875

Jonathan Seidel
610-948-5175
www.jkseidel.com

www.marariley.net

www.tapelooms.com

EBay and other online auction sites

Pinterest, hand weaving pages

Ravelry, handwoven tape page

Museum shops (some periodically sell tape looms). See Appendix 3.

Scandinavian Band Weaving

"The Sami People and Their Weaving," Susan J. Foulkes, *Handwoven Magazine,* Mar./Apr. 2013.
www.weavezine.com/content/Scandinavian-tape-looms

Coverlet Books that Discuss Floor Loom Fringe Weaving

Crosson, Janet Gray. *Point Work Coverlets.* Lancaster, PA: Old Fibers, Weavers & Coverlets, 1999.

Angstadt, John P. *Cloths and Coverlets: The Angstadt Weavers.* Lititz, PA: Self published, 2002

Jarvis, Helen N. *Weaving a Traditional Coverlet.* Loveland, CO: Interweave Press, 1989.

Appendix 3

Suggested Museums with Tape Collections

Daniel Boone Homestead
400 Daniel Boone Road
Birdsboro, PA 19508
610-582-4900
www.danielboonehomestead.org

Ephrata Cloister
632 West Main Street
Ephrata, PA 17527
717-733-6600
www.ephratacloister.org

Goschenhoppen Museum
116 Gravel Pike
Green Lane, PA 18054
215-234-8953
www.goschenhoppen.org

Hans Herr House and Museum
1849 Hans Herr Drive, Willow Street
717-464-4438
www.hansherr.org

Hagley Museum
Route 141
Wilmington, DE
302-658-2400
www.hagley.org

Hancock Shaker Village
PO Box 898
Pittsfield, MA 01202
413-443-0188
www.hsv.org

LancasterHistory.org
230 North President Avenue
Lancaster, PA 17603
717-392-4633
www.lancasterhistory.org

Landis Valley Village and Farm Museum
2451 Kissel Hill Road
Lancaster, PA 17601
717-569-0401
www.landisvalleymuseum.org

Mennonite Historical Society
2215 Millstream Rd
Lancaster, PA 17602
717-393-9745
www.lmhs.org

Mercer Museum
84 South Pine Street
Doylestown, PA 18901
215-345-0210
www.mercermuseum.org

Old Sturbridge Village
1 Old Sturbridge Village Road
Sturbridge, MA 01566
508-347-3362
www.osv.org

Peter Wentz Farmstead
Shearer Road
Worcester, PA 19490
610-584-5104
www.peterwentzfarmsteadsociety.org

Schwenkfelder Library and Heritage Center
105 Seminary Street
Pennsburg, PA 18073-1898
215-679-3103
www.schwenkfelder.com

Colonial Williamsburg
PO Box 1776
Williamsburg, VA 23187
877-996-4940
www.colonialwilliamsburg.com

Winterthur
5105 Kennett Pike (Route 52)
Winterthur, DE 19735
302-888-4600
www.winterthur.org

Appendix 4

Draft and Chart Templates
These templates may be useful in creating your
own tape patterns.

Warp Color Draft

Warp Color Draft ⟶

HOLE																							
SLOT																							

Tape Pattern Chart

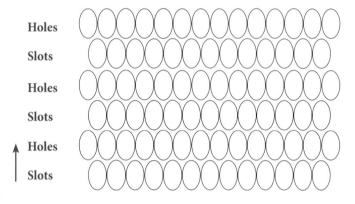

Holes

Slots

Holes

Slots

Holes

Slots

Notes

Introduction
1. Ellen J. Gehret, *Rural Pennsylvania Clothing* (York, PA: George Shumway Publisher, 1976), 239.

Chapter 1
1. Janet Crosson, foreword to *Rural Pennsylvania Clothing*, by Ellen J. Gehret (York, PA: George Shumway Publisher, 1976), 16.
2. Alice Morse Earle, *Home Life in Colonial Days* (Stockbridge, MA: Berkshire House Publishers, 1898), 167.
3. Linda Eaton, Textile Curator, Winterthur Museum, Winterthur, DE, interview with author, June 2, 2015.
4. Alice Morse Earle, *Home Life in Colonial Days* (Stockbridge, MA: Berkshire House Publishers, 1898), 225.
5. Aline Saarinen, "Mr. and Mrs. Thomas Mifflin," *McCalls*, 1967.
6. Monica D. Spiese, *Pennsylvania German Textile and Dye Plants* (Lancaster, PA: Landis Valley Village and Farm Museum, 1993), 19.
7. Ellen J. Gehret, *Rural Pennsylvania Clothing* (York, PA: George Shumway Publisher, 1976), 239.
8. Ibid.
9. Ibid., 16.
10. Ibid., 183.
11. Eleanor Bittle, "The Tape Lady," Gilbertsville, PA, interview with author, May 2, 2015.
12. Ellen J. Gehret, *Rural Pennsylvania Clothing* (York, PA: George Shumway Publisher, 1976), 64.
13. Ibid., 73.
14. Ibid., 75.
15. Ibid., 57.
16. Tandy Hersh and Charles Hersh, *Cloth and Costume, 1750 to 1800, Cumberland County, Pennsylvania* (Carlisle, PA: Cumberland County Historical Society, 1995), 61.
17. Ellen J. Gehret, *Rural Pennsylvania Clothing* (York, PA: George Shumway Publisher, 1976), 58.
18. Ibid., 239.
19. Ibid., 139.
20. John F. Watson, *Annals of Philadelphia and Pennsylvania in the Olden Times,* vol. 1 (Philadelphia, 1857), 193, quoted in *Rural Pennsylvania Clothing*, by Ellen J. Gehret (York, PA: George Shumway Publisher, 1976), 262.
21. Ibid.
22. Ellen J. Gehret in cooperation with Tandy Hersh, Alan G. Keyser, and Frederick S. Weiser, *This Is the Way I Pass My Time* (Kutztown, PA: The Pennsylvania German Society, 1985), 8.
23. Ibid., 246.
24. Marion L. Channing, *The Textile Tools of Colonial Homes* (Marion, MA.: self published, 1969, 1971), 58.
25. Alice Morse Earle, *Home Life in Colonial Days* (Stockbridge, MA: Berkshire House Publishers, 1898), 239.
26. Lesley Herzberg, Hancock Shaker Village, interview with author, June 22, 2015.
27. Clarke E. Hess, *Mennonite Arts* (Atglen, PA: Schiffer Publishing, Ltd., 2002), 139.
28. "Red" tape research, The British National Archives, London, England, www.nationalarchives.gov.uk.
29. Jenny Dean, *Wild Color* (London: Octopus Publishing Group Ltd., 1999, 2010), 17.
30. Mary Jane Myers, Quality Administrator, Wayne Mills Company, Philadelphia, PA, interview with author, Sept. 24, 2014.

Chapter 2
1. Lucille Long, *Anna Elizabeth* (Elgin, IL: Brethren Publishing House, 1942), 134.
2. Alice Morse Earle, *Home Life in Colonial Days* (Stockbridge, MA: Berkshire House Publishers, 1898), 225.
3. Wendy Christie and Alan G. Keyser, Cocalico Creek Country Store, Stevens, PA, interviews with author, Sept. 14, 2013.
4. Regina Britten, *Tape Loom Weaving Simplified* (Torrington, CT: self published, 2013), 12.
5. Eleanor Bittle, "The Tape Lady," Gilbertsville, PA, interview with author, May 12, 2015.
6. Jonathan Seidel, tape loom maker, Royersford, PA, interview with author, Aug. 20, 2009.

Chapter 3

1. Ellen J. Gehret and Alan G. Keyser, *Homespun Textile Traditions of the Pennsylvania Germans* (Harrisburg, PA: Pennsylvania Historical and Museum Commission, 1976), 2.
2. Ibid., 3.
3. Ibid., 2.
4. Ellen J. Gehret, *Rural Pennsylvania Clothing* (York, PA: George Shumway Publisher, 1976), 242.
5. Monica D. Spiese, *Pennsylvania German Textile and Dye Plants* (Lancaster, PA: Landis Valley Village and Farm Museum, 1993), 18.
6. Les Stark, *Hempstone Heritage I* (Morgantown, PA: Masthof Press, 2005), 4.
7. Ibid., 7.
8. Ibid., 8.
9. Ibid., 36.
10. Eleanor Bittle, "The Tape Lady," Gilbertsville, PA, interview with author, May 12, 2015.
11. Ellen J. Gehret and Alan G. Keyser, *Homespun Textile Traditions of the Pennsylvania Germans* (Harrisburg, PA: Pennsylvania Historical and Museum Commission, 1976), 3.
12. Patricia Baines, *Linen, Hand Spinning and Weaving* (London: B. T. Batsford Ltd., 1989), 174.
13. Eleanor Bittle, "The Tape Lady," Gilbertsville, PA, interview with author, May 12, 2015.
14. Ellen J. Gehret and Alan G. Keyser, *Homespun Textile Traditions of the Pennsylvania Germans* (Harrisburg, PA: Pennsylvania Historical and Museum Commission, 1976), 4.
15. Ellen J. Gehret, *Rural Pennsylvania Clothing* (York, PA: George Shumway Publisher, 1976), 225.
16. Jenny Dean, *Wild Color* (London: Octopus Publishing Group Ltd., 1999, 2010), 124.
17. Amy Butler Greenfield, *A Perfect Red* (New York: HarperCollins, 2005), 28.
18. Ibid., 76.
19. Eleanor Bittle, "The Tape Lady," Gilbertsville, PA, interview with author, May 12, 2015.

Chapter 4

1. Eleanor Bittle, "The Tape Lady," Gilbertsville, PA, interview with author, May 12, 2015.
2. Alan G. Keyser, Cocalico Creek Country Store, Stevens, PA, interview with author, Sept. 14, 2013.
3. Ellen J. Gehret, *Rural Pennsylvania Clothing* (York, PA: George Shumway Publisher, 1976), 242.
4. Ibid.
5. Eleanor Bittle, "The Tape Lady," Gilbertsville, PA, interview with author, May 12, 2015.
6. Evelyn Neher, *Inkle* (Guilford, CT: self published, 1974), 209.
7. Gay McGeary, coverlet weaver, Carlisle, PA, interview, with author, April 26, 2015.
8. Janet Gray Crosson, *Point Work Coverlets* (Lancaster, PA: Old Fibers, Weavers & Coverlets, 1999), 6.
9. Ibid., 6
10. Gay McGeary, coverlet weaver, Carlisle, PA, interview, with author, April 26, 2015.
11. Ibid.
12. Eleanor Bittle, "The Tape Lady," Gilbertsville, PA, interview with author, May 12, 2015.
13. Ibid.
14. Ibid.
15. Ellen J. Gehret, *Rural Pennsylvania Clothing* (York, PA: George Shumway Publisher, 1976), 242.
16. Clarke E. Hess, *Mennonite Arts* (Atglen, PA: Schiffer Publishing, Ltd., 2002), 42.
17. Eleanor Bittle, "The Tape Lady," Gilbertsville, PA, interview with author, May 12, 2015.

Chapter 5

1. Elizabeth Bertheaud, Director, Ephrata Cloister, Ephrata, PA, interview with author, Sept. 20, 2014.

Chapter 7

1. Evelyn Neher, *Inkle* (Guilford, CT: self published, 1974), 203.
2. Chris Yovino, Hagley Museum, Wilmington, DE, interview with author, June 23, 2015.

Weaving Glossary

Beaming Up: In the warping process, the winding of the warp threads onto the back roller or reel.

Balanced Plain Weave or Tabby: The warp and weft threads are all equal distanced between each other. Not as strong as a warp-faced weave for tape.

Belt Shuttle: The tool used to hold the weft threads and weave across the warp threads. The shuttle should have a clean, beveled edge on one side, for beating in the weft.

Cross: When measuring the warp threads on the warping board, the "figure 8" or *cross* created at top dowels. The cross keeps the long warp threads in order, preventing tangles when feeding them into the rigid heddle.

Draft: The map or guide of the warp color placement, creating the pattern.

Draw-In: In the weaving process, the pulling in of the selvages with the weft thread, too tightly.

Guide String: A thread that is measured to the length of the weaving project and wrapped around the appropriate dowels on a warping board. Easier to see if a contrasting color from the warp threads.

Leader Cord: A strong cord tied to a warp bundle behind a paddle loom. It is tied to a pole to secure it.

Leader Thread: A strong thread tied to the roller of a box or floor tape loom. It is attached to the bundle of warp threads to wind on the warp. A leader thread is not necessary to use on a reel.

Lease Sticks: Two cardboard or thin wooden sticks with holes in each end, to keep them tied together. They are used to hold the warp thread *cross* when feeding the warps into the rigid heddle.

Mercerized Cotton: This cotton is stronger and shinier than un-mercerized cotton, due to its processing.

Ratchet and Pawl Brake System: Working together as a brake, the ratchet is a round, notched wooden circle and the pawl acts as the handle, to lock the ratchet in place. Some tape looms have one set and others have two sets, one in the back and one in front of the rigid heddle.

Reel: One of the two styles of back beams for the warp threads to be wound on to for collecting the length. It is more elaborately built than a roller, but is easier to use.

Rigid Heddle: The flat, wooden frame used to move the warp threads up and down. It contains measured holes across, with long vertical slots in between each hole. The warp threads going through the holes are stationary, while the warp threads fed through the slots move up or down, to change the shed, as the weaving takes place.

Roller: One of the two styles of back beams for collecting the length of warp threads. A large smooth dowel, it winds on the length of warp threads.

Row or Shot: Weaving the weft through a shed, with a shuttle.

Selvages: The edges or sides of the woven tape cloth.

Shed: One of two openings in the warp threads for the shuttle to pass through.

Tape: A long narrow band of cloth, woven in a warp-faced weave structure, with many uses.

T-Pin: A long pin with a T shape at the end of it. It can be used for fixing a broken warp thread or other issues in the weaving process.

Warp Threads: The first long threads that are fed through the loom. It is important that they be smooth and strong, since they do most of the work in the weaving process.

Warp: This word has several different meanings. It can mean one warp thread, a group of warp threads, or the verb, to warp the loom.

Warp-Faced Plain Weave: This can be confusing, but the term refers to a warp-faced weave structure. Plain weave, here, means the use of two sheds in the weaving process.

Warp-Faced Weave Structure: The only threads that are seen are the warp threads. The weft pulls the many warp threads snug and close to each other, with every woven row, creating a strong woven cloth. The weft is hidden inside of the warp threads, only seen peaking out at the selvages.

Web: The body of the woven tape, on the loom.

Weft: Wrapped on the shuttle, this thread is woven through the warp threads, from selvage to selvage.

Bibliography

Baines, Patricia. *Linen, Hand Spinning and Weaving.* London: B.T. Batsford Ltd, 1989.

The British National Archives, London, England, "red tape" historic data, www.nationalarchives.gov.uk.

Britton, Regina. *Tape Loom Weaving Simplified.* Torrington, CT: self published, 2013.

Channing, Marion L. *The Textile Tools of Colonial Homes.* Marion, MA: self published, 1969, 1971.

Crosson, Janet Gray. *Point Work Coverlets.* Lancaster, PA: Old Fibers, Weavers & Coverlets, 1999.

Dean, Jenny. *Wild Color.* London: Octopus Publishing Group Ltd., 1999, 2010.

Earle, Alice Morse. *Home Life in Colonial Days.* Stockbridge, MA: Berkshire House Publishers, 1898.

Edwin Miller Fogel. *Beliefs and Superstions of the Pennsylvania Germans.* Philadephia: 1915.

Gehret, Ellen J. *Rural Pennsylvania Clothing.* York, PA: George Shumway Publisher, 1976.

Gehret, Ellen J., in cooperation with Tandy Hersh, Alan G. Keyser, and Frederick S. Weiser. *This Is the Way I Pass My Time.* Kutztown, PA: The Pennsylvania German Society, 1985.

Gehret, Ellen J. and Alan G. Keyser. *Homespun Textile Traditions of the Pennsylvania Germans.* Harrisburg, PA: Pennsylvania Historical and Museum Commission, 1976.

Greenfield, Amy Butler. *A Perfect Red.* New York, NY: HarperCollins Publishers, Inc., 2005.

Hersh, Tandy, and Charles Hersh. *Cloth and Costume, 1750 to 1800, Cumberland County, Pennsylvania.* Carlisle, PA: Cumberland County Historical Society, 1995.

Hess, Clarke E. *Mennonite Arts.* Atglen, PA: Schiffer Publishing Ltd., 2002.

Long, Lucille. *Anna Elizabeth.* Elgin, IL: Brethren Publishing House, 1942.

Neher, Evelyn. *Inkle.* Guilford, CT: self published, 1974.

Saarinen, Aline. "Mr. and Mrs. Thomas Mifflin," *McCalls*, 1967.

Spiese, Monica D. *Pennsylvania German Textile and Dye Plants.* Lancaster, PA: Landis Valley Village and Farm Museum, 1993.

Stark, Les. *Hempstone Heritage I.* Morgantown, PA: Masthof Press, 2005.

Interviews

Elizabeth Bertheaud, Director of the Ephrata Cloister, Ephrata, PA. Sept. 20, 2014.

Eleanor Bittle, "The Tape Lady," Gilbertsville, PA. May 12, 2015

Wendy Christie, Cocalico Creek Country Store, Stevens, PA. April 14, 2013.

Linda Eaton, Textile Curator, Winterthur Museum, Winterthur, DE. June 2, 2015.

Lesley Herzberg, Hancock Shaker Village, Pittsfield, MA. June 22, 2015.

Alan G. Keyser, Cocalico Creek Country Store, Stevens, PA. April 14, 2013.

Gay McGeary, coverlet weaver, Carlisle, PA. April 26, 2015.

Mary Jane Myers, Quality Administrator, Wayne Mills Company, Philadelphia, PA. Sept. 24, 2014.

Candace Perry, Schwenkfelder Library and Heritage Center, Pennsburg, PA. July 22, 2015.

Jennifer Royer, Landis Valley Village and Farm Museum, Lancaster, PA. July 8, 2015.

Jonathan Seidel, Royersford, PA. Aug. 20, 2009.

Chris Yovino, Hagley Museum, Wilmington, DE. June 23, 2015.

OTHER SCHIFFER BOOKS ON RELATED SUBJECTS

Norwegian Pick-Up Bandweaving

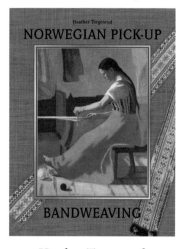

Heather Torgenrud
ISBN 978-0-7643-4751-1

Weaving Shaker Rugs
Traditional Techniques to Create Beautiful Reproduction Rugs and Tapes

Mary Elva Congleton Erf
ISBN 978-0-7643-4907-2